"The market for profession[al] dramatically in the last co[u...] no longer enough to win [...] *The Invisible Market* shows *professionals how to be-* come experts on their clients to build long lasting and profitable partnerships. "
— John Viola - Vice President,
Senior Account Executive,
Merrill Lynch Capital

"Reading **Winning In The Invisible Market** made me recognize some of the bad habits that I have fallen into, and reminded me that the "professional" part of "professional services" really means something. "
— Jonathan Whitehead -
Managing Director, BearingPoint

"Bob Potter's insights into the less understood proc-ess of selling professional services are unique and powerful. **Winning in the Invisible Market** is the new paradigm for selling professional services. "
— Gunnar Branson - Former Chief
Marketing Officer, Heller Financial

"Bob Potter thinks and writes clearly—a valuable asset in our fast paced business world. **Winning In The Invisible Market** focuses your attention on the eminently practical. What really works? Why? That's the key to success. "
— Peter Pike - CEO, PikeNet

"We thought we knew how to sell because we were good at what we did. **Winning In The Invisible Market** showed us how to proactively access new re-lationships, build value and get paid for it. It gave us the road map and navigation tools to win. "
— Kathy Huber - President,
Market Insite Group

*"Great sales strategy and tactics can be developed by mere mortals. **Winning In The Invisible Market** showed me how to create the business instead of wait for the business. That is critical in this market."*

-- Scott Reay - Executive Vice President,
Business Development and Sales,
BCCI Construction

*"Acquiring new clients has never been more difficult. Tightly aligning your message and approach with potential clients' needs and situation is not an option - it's a prerequisite today. **Winning In The Invisible Market** shows how service providers can prosper even in tough markets. A must read for survival in your profession."*

--Brian Bouren - Former Chief
Marketing Officer, NerveWire, Inc.

*"Being in the construction industry, I was stuck in the old way of marketing and sales. **Winning In The Invisible Market** changed my approach to potential new clients and, more importantly, my existing clients. Now my clients make faster decisions, and they are more committed as partners."*

-- Brian A Trainor - President,
Trainor Commercial Construction

*"**Winning In The Invisible Market** offers invaluable insight on the power of aligning to client interests to create win-win engagements."*

-- Lindsay Beaman - President, Corporate
& Marketing Communications, Inc.

WINNING
IN THE
INVISIBLE
MARKET

A GUIDE TO SELLING PROFESSIONAL
SERVICES IN TURBULENT TIMES

By Robert A. Potter

Dedication

To my wife, Amy, and sons, Michael and Matthew

Winning Acknowledgements

Thanks to the colleagues, clients, service leaders, friends and family who shared their time and knowledge to make this book possible.

Karen Appleton - Director of Business Development, Orrick
John Arndt - Advertising representative, Latitude 38
Arthur Barrett - Former President, Franchise Associates
Lindsay Beaman - President, Corporate & Marketing Communications, Inc.
Brian Bouren - Former Chief Marketing Officer, NerveWire, Inc.
Rick Bragdon - President, Idiom Brand Identity
Gunnar Branson - Former Chief Marketing Officer, Heller Financial
Christopher Browne, CFA - Manager, Strategy and Business Development, Autodesk, Inc.
W. Scott Bumpas - Vice Chairman, Fischer & Company
Carol M. Donahue - Director of Business Development, Babson Executive Education
Peter Dubner - Friend
Ross Dove - Chairman of the Board, CEO, DoveBid
Janet L. Fall - CEO, Semper Group
Douglas P. Frye - President & CEO, Colliers International
Thomas S. Fischer - Former Partner, Accenture
George Gallagher - Regional Director, CoStar Group, Inc.
Jay M. Gentry - President, CCT Inc.
Ronald E. Gerevas - Partner & former CEO, Heidrick & Struggles
David Golden - Managing Director, J.P. Morgan Chase
James S. Greene - Vice President, Global Financial Services, Cap Gemini Ernst & Young, U.S. LLC
Richard E Hake - President, Kipling Capital, Inc.
Arthur P. Hall - Sr. Managing Director, Global Business Integration, Cushman & Wakefield
Christopher J. Healey - Partner, Luce, Forward, Hamilton & Scripps
John P. Hoskins - Co Founder - Advantage Performance Group
Kathy Huber - President, Market Insite Group
Tony Hughes - Managing Director, Salomon Smith Barney
Gil Judson - Goddu-Henderson-Judson Consulting, Inc.
James C. Kennedy - Senior Vice President, Computer Sciences Corporation
Mike Krenn - Managing Director, Venture Pipeline Group, Grey Carey
Reinhard Ludke - Vice President, Creegan + D'Angelo
Chad Lynch - Business Development Manager, Deloitte & Touche LLP
John Mahoney - Sr. Vice President, Risk & Asset Management, Storage USA
Andy Mathieson - President, Fairview Capital
Mark A. McLaughlin - President, McLaughlin Ventures
Dennis F. Murphy - P.E., Senior Vice President, Coleman Consulting Group
Bill Nowacki - Managing Director, Fair, Isaac and Company Inc.

Jamie Pfaff - Group Creative Director, Corbett Healthcare Communications
Peter Pike - President, PikeNet
Steve Piccone - Vice President, Sales Manager, Merrill Corporation
Donald A. Potter - Management Consultant, Potter Consulting
Donald V. Potter - CEO, StrategyStreet.com
Mary Jo Potter - Senior officer, global consulting firm
Richard J Potter - Director, Vital Strategic Client Program, Deloitte Consulting
Conrad Prusak - President, Ethos Consulting
Scott Reay - Executive Vice President, Business Development and Sales, BCCI Construction
Tom Rodenhauser - President, Consulting Information Services, LLC
Michael Roster - Executive Vice President and General Counsel, Golden West Financial Corporation
Juergen Rottler - Vice President, Marketing, Strategy & Alliances, HP Services
Joseph B. Rubin - Partner, Ernst & Young LLP
Peter Ruggiero - Principal, Prudential Real Estate Investors
Susan Shultis - FSA
Larry Smith - Director of Strategy, Levick Strategic Communications LLC
Andrea Snedeker - Marketing & Business Development Manager, Townsend and Townsend and Crew
Michael Solomon - Entrepreneur, advisor and investor
Matthew Slepin - Partner, Heidrick & Struggles
Brian Sprague - Associate Partner, Accenture
Brian A Trainor - President Trainor Commercial Construction
John Viola - Vice President, Senior Account Executive, Merrill Lynch Capital
Bruce Zev Weissberg - CEO, ChicagoLand Commissary, LLC
John C. Wills - President/CEO, FLI, Incorporated
Jonathan Whitehead - Managing Director, BearingPoint
Dan Winey - VP & Managing Principal, Gensler
Jeanne Yocum - Tuscarora Communications, Ltd.
Amy Zinman - Manager of Attorney Professional Development, Nixon Peabody LLP

Table of Contents

Introduction

R emember when your biggest challenge was to service a growing list of clients without working more than 80 hours a week? When the only worry your firm had was finding, hiring, retaining and locating all of the new professionals to meet the insatiable demand for your services? When "business development" consisted of answering the phone, showing off capabilities with that PowerPoint presentation and tossing in a boilerplate proposal? Do you remember "firing" unprofitable clients?

How things have changed.

The technology bust, terrorist attacks, war overseas and a seemingly endless parade of corporate scandals have converged to create a "perfect storm" of economic adversity. Those who earn their living by selling professional services are now facing the most challenging business environment in more than a generation. Incomes have been slashed and many have been "right-sized" out of a job.

Every day now I hear a drumbeat of despair from professional services providers competing for their share of a much smaller and hyper-competitive new business pie.

"They won't even meet with me."

"The decision has been put on hold indefinitely."

"Everything is price, price, price."

"There is no way I can make my numbers."

However dire the situation may seem, plenty of business is still out there. In fact, some professionals are not only surviving in this turbulent market; they are prospering. What are these professionals doing to win more of the existing business? What are they doing to create new business? That is what I wanted to find out in order to help my own professional services clients survive the worst downturn in a generation. *Winning in the Invisible Market* is the result of that effort.

I have been a professional services provider for 25 years, working as an investment banker, sales and marketing executive, CEO, author and consultant. Over the course of my career, I have opened new markets in the U.S., Mexico, Australia and Asia. Several years ago, I sold a successful financial services company that I had co-founded and started an advisory firm to help other service companies penetrate new markets and win new business.

When demand for professional services started to decline in 2000, I began searching for resources to help my clients weather the coming storm. I quickly discovered that although there were hundreds of books about selling, most were written for selling products – not for selling top-level professional services.

The books that did target services tended to rehash product-selling techniques. These resources simply weren't appropriate for service-provider executives whose clients were senior executives making multi-million dollar decisions that affect careers and companies.

I wanted to understand how successful service providers were surviving the worst downturn in a generation and pass that knowledge onto my client base. I decided to go straight to the source. I spent the better part of two years interviewing successful service providers to find out what they do differently to prosper in tough markets. I also talked to their clients to learn how and why they made the decision to use an outside service and to hire the particular service provider they did.

I discovered that the most successful service providers do approach the market quite differently. How? They create new business before their competitors have an opportunity to compete. *They are winning business when it is still invisible to the rest of the market.*

The objective of *Winning in the Invisible Market* is to give you a map and navigation tools to win in the invisible market and to actually prosper during turbulent times. The book takes the buying and selling patterns gleaned from both top sales leaders and their clients and converts them into a logical and learnable process and skills that will enable you to incorporate its powerful content into your day-to-day business development activities. It will help you sell less, win more and have more control over this critical part of your career no matter what the market does.

A word of warning: this book is not a light read. Out of respect for your limited time, I have kept it as short as possible, but the content does include complex concepts that will require your diligence and practice to master. I have included a summary at the beginning of each chapter and a glossary of terms and concepts at the end of each chapter to help you preview and review key words and ideas as we work through the material.

The approach of the book is not to simply prescribe what you should do to become more effective at selling in the invisible market. Instead, it encourages you to develop **strategic empathy** – a thorough understanding of the rational and emotional reasons and processes that your prospective clients use when they decide to use your services or when they choose one service provider over another. The better you understand how and why potential clients make such decisions, the more effectively you can align your service, strategy and recommendations with the prospect's motivation and decision-making process.

You will use strategic empathy to create your own unique selling response that parallels your potential client's purpose and process. This will make it easier and more comfortable for a prospective client to commit to your recommendations. Prospects will be more willing to meet with you, share problems and explore solutions with you, make faster decisions, choose you over competitors more often and be more committed to working closely with you to assure the success of the engagement.

Successful engagements create delighted clients, and delighted clients willingly become your surrogate sales force. They give you more follow-on business and refer you to new prospects. This means you spend less time selling and more time helping your clients achieve their objectives. To begin our exploration of strategic empathy, let's look at who is winning the business now and why these professionals are meeting with success while others flounder.

Part I:
Winning in the Invisible Market:
Supporting the Transformation Decision

B efore they hire you, potential clients make *two decisions.* They decide to change or transform some part of their business (the transformation decision), and then they choose you among alternatives to help them make the desired change (the service provider decision). Successful professional service providers win the service provider decision in the visible market by supporting the transformation decision in the invisible market. In Part I we will focus on winning in the invisible market using a strategy I call **Value Mining** to find and align to your prospective client's motivation and resistance to change. In Part II we will focus on winning the service provider decision in the visible market using a strategy I call **Preference Value Mining** to find and align to the prospective client's rational and emotional comparison criteria.

Chapter 1

Who's Winning Now?
Becoming the Preferred
or the Sole Provider

Pursuing new business exclusively in the visible market – the portion of the market where companies are actively and openly looking for a service provider – is a dead end strategy in this economy. The only way to win in these turbulent times is to become the sole or preferred provider, and that can only happen by · venturing into the invisible market and engaging clients before they look for service providers. The objective of Winning In The Invisible Market is to give you a map and navigation tools to penetrate and create new business in the invisible market.

The Visible Winners

The head of a health care consulting practice was faced with a dramatic downturn in business and asked me to help his team win in competitive "bake-offs." I suggested that we work on tactics to reduce or eliminate competition by engaging prospective clients *before* they made the decision to use a consultant. The CEO responded that this approach would be a waste of time because all business today was competitive.

I later asked a board member of a major health care system

about their use of consultants. She told me that their last eight engagements were sole-sourced, meaning that they did not conduct a competitive search before hiring a consultant.

How could two players from the same industry hold such divergent views of how outside professionals are hired? The answer: if you wait for clients to approach you with Requests for Proposals (RFPs) or Statements of Qualifications (SOQs), all of the potential business you see *is* competitively bid. In reality, the percentage of business that is truly competitive is much less than it appears.

The **visible market** – the portion of the market comprised of companies actively and openly looking for a service provider – represents only the tip of the opportunity iceberg as shown in the graphic below.

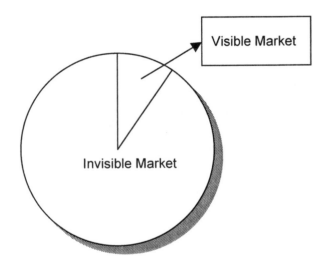

By the time companies enter your field of vision by taking proactive steps to hire an outside professional – asking for proposals, statements of qualifications or price quotes – your competition has probably already been there. Yes, the prospects are qualified; you can be assured they are actively seeking the type of services you provide. But unfortunately, in most cases, the prospect already has a **preferred provider** who usually wins the business.

If you are not the preferred provider, the deck is stacked against you. As the diagram below demonstrates, only a small portion of the opportunities in the visible market are truly competitive, further narrowing your market if you focus only on those companies that are visibly active.

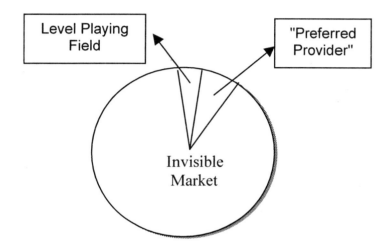

The Invisible Winners

In addition to the visible and invisible markets, there is also an **invisible active market** where companies are quietly choosing service providers on a sole-source basis. The size of this market varies in different industries but, as the health care example above demonstrates, it is always larger than service providers suspect.

Take, for instance, the U.S. federal government, which is the largest consumer of business services. Everyone knows that government contracts are competitively bid, right? Look again. More than half of all federal service contracts are sole sourced.[*] And, if you take a closer look at the remaining "competitive" engagements, you'll see that a preferred bidder wins the majority of those.

By the time a company decides to seek outside services and moves into the visible market, it is reaching the end of a multiphase decision-making process. They have already identified and assessed a problem and envisioned and built internal consensus on a solution. Of primary importance to you, they often have a preferred service provider in mind – a provider who began supporting them before the project became "visible." In all likelihood, this preferred service provider will be chosen to help the prospect reach the envisioned solution.

So, where should you put your sales efforts?

Clearly, you want to become the preferred or sole source provider because these positions offer higher margins, higher hit rates and more committed and supportive clients. But to do this, you will have to venture into the invisible market and engage companies earlier in their decision-making process and establish your value before they start comparing service providers.

By building a value relationship with the prospect earlier in the process, you can win more exclusive business or establish a competitive advantage as a preferred provider. But venturing into the invisible market is easier said than done.

The Value Gap: *Undervalued and Unappreciated*

The invisible market is where all preferred or sole-sourced business is created. But it can be a forbidding place, full of potential clients who don't know you, don't know they need you and don't know how your services differ from those offered by your competitors.

The reason selling professional services can be so difficult, and sometimes downright painful, in the invisible market is that potential clients cannot possibly understand or fully appreciate all that you can do for them before you actually do it. And, unfortunately, if companies do not value you before the service is performed, then they won't be inclined to use your services, choose you over alternative providers or pay what you're worth. They may not even be willing to meet with you.

This is what I call a **value gap** – the difference between a prospect's perceptions of the value of services you offer and the actual value you can deliver. Anyone who has attempted to access and acquire new clients knows that initially the value gap can be a fairly wide chasm. What's more, because the terms of your engagement are set *before* you provide the service, you inevitably fight the value gap at each stage of the business development process.

There are two types of value gaps that you will encounter: the *service* value gap and the *preference* value gap. A **service value gap** *occurs in the invisible market* when the potential client has no perceived need or sense of urgency for the services you offer. For instance, a potential client may not yet be convinced that his or her company has a problem and therefore isn't in the market for your services right now. Perhaps the prospect has already addressed the problem or been burned in the past, making the risk of taking new action too great. Or perhaps the prospect doesn't understand or believe your solution. Maybe they just don't have the authority, consensus or resources to act right now. All of these are examples of service value gaps.

A **preference value gap** *occurs in the visible market* after the prospect has made the decision to use a service but chooses to use one of your competitors to deliver that service. A preference value gap arises when the potential client does not understand or appreciate what makes your service different and better than alternatives.

Whatever the reason, when faced with a value gap, you are operating in a world in which you are unappreciated and undervalued. This is unpleasant both professionally and personally. The invisible market is where the biggest value gaps are, and it is replete with rejection and wasted time. But, it is also the only place to become a preferred or sole provider.

So the choice is to continue to bang your head against the wall competing for a piece of the decreasing visible market pie or get ready to win in the invisible market. Naturally, before entering such unexplored territory, you will want to understand how to gain access, close value gaps, determine who is going to make a decision, and then be able to shepherd that decision as a preferred or sole provider.

The next step in developing **strategic empathy** is to understand how clients decide to use outside professional services. We'll look at that in Chapter 2.

*Stanberry, Scott A., *Federal Contracting Made Easy*, Management Concepts, Inc., January 2001.

Chapter 1:
Glossary of Terms and Key Concepts

Strategic Empathy - An understanding of the rational and emotional motivation and process that your prospective clients use when they make a decision to use a service and when they choose one service provider over another. The more you understand how and why potential clients make both decisions, the more you can "naturally" align your service, strategy and presentation to be in sync with your prospect's process and motivation.

Visible Market - The portion of the market comprised of companies actively and openly seeking a service provider. By the time companies enter your field of vision by taking proactive steps to hire an outside professional – asking for proposals, statements of qualifications or price quotes – it is likely that your competition has already been there.

Invisible Market - The majority of the market, which consists of companies not actively and openly looking for a service provider. Prospects in the invisible market may be at an earlier decision stage, may have already addressed a problem or may not have the motivation or resources to address a problem.

Invisible Active Market - The portion of the market where companies are quietly choosing service providers on a sole-source basis. The size of this market varies in different industries, but it is almost always larger than service providers suspect.

Preferred Provider - A favored competitor among alternative service providers. By the time a company decides to seek outside services, it frequently has a service provider in mind – often a provider who began supporting them before the project became "visible." In all likelihood, this provider will be chosen to help the prospect reach an envisioned solution that the pre-ferred provider helped to create.

Sole Provider - A firm chosen without competition. In other words, the client did not conduct a competitive search and evaluation before hiring the provider. Preferred or sole-source provider positions offer higher margins, higher hit rates and more committed and supportive clients.

Value Gap - The difference between a prospect's percep-tion of the value of the services you offer and the actual value you can deliver. If companies do not value you before the ser-vice is performed, then they won't be inclined to meet with you, use your services, choose you over alternatives or pay what you're worth.

Service Value Gap - Occurs in the invisible market when the potential client has no perceived need or urgency for the services you offer.

Preference Value Gap - Occurs in the visible market when the prospect has made the decision to use a service but prefers a competitor. The potential client does not understand or appreci-ate what makes your service different and better than alternatives.

Chapter 2

The Invisible Market Decision:
Understanding the Prospect's Transformation Decision

B efore they hire you, potential clients make *two decisions.* They decide to transform some part of their business (the transformation decision), and then they choose you among alternatives to help them make the desired change.

In this chapter, you will see that all transformation decisions have three components: 1) **motivation** to leave current practices, 2) a **vision** of better future state, and 3) a reliable **path** to achieve the vision. Together, these three steps are called **Transformation MVP**.

The more you know about your client's motivation, vision and path, the more likely you are to position your service, strategy and message in a way that builds value and preference in the mind of the client.

When service providers think about winning business, they tend to focus on winning the service provider decision by being chosen over competitors. But that is not where the process of hiring a service provider really begins. Before potential clients make the service provider choice, they must first decide to make a change. As a professional service provider, the business problems you solve are typically complex. These problems require prospective clients to commit to making a significant change – a **Transformation Decision**.

Without the transformation decision, the prospect has no need to make a service provider decision. Companies don't choose an integration consultant until they decide to integrate their computer and software systems. They don't need an attorney until they decide to take legal action. They don't need an architect until they decide to build a building.

The active market is that portion of the market that is making a service provider decision. The rest of the market, the invisible inactive market, is either in an earlier stage of the transformation decision or remains dormant.

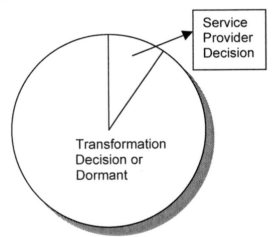

Service Provider Decision

Transformation Decision or Dormant

Let's explore the invisible market, where you have the greatest opportunity to achieve your goal of becoming the preferred or exclusive provider. In this market, you are not only asking companies to choose *you*; you are asking them to choose *change*. You are inviting them to make a decision to transform.

I'll return to the visible market later in the book to review how companies make service provider decisions, and I'll also show you how to win once there is competition. First, I'd like to take you inside the transformation decision.

Understanding Transformation MVP:
Motivation, Vision and Path to Resolution

A transformational decision is an executive decision that has a major impact on a company. It is a decision to abandon current practices in favor of a new approach; it is a commitment to a new strategy, process, team, or resource allocation.

Transformation decisions are caused when business plans and objectives meet the reality of a continuously changing market. Changing conditions such as new information, new competitors, changes in demand, technology advances, or legal challenges throw existing plans and methods out of sync, threatening the success of the organization.

Transformation decisions have three critical components: Motivation (M), Vision (V) and Path to Resolution (P). I refer to the process as **Transformation MVP**, which includes a *motivation* to leave current practices, a clear *vision* of a better future situation and a reliable *path* to resolve the problem and attain the vision.

Transformation MVP

Motivation	*Vision*	*Path to Resolution*
Problems?	Objectives?	Effort?
Causes?	Alternatives?	Disruption?
Status quo	Rewards?	Risk?
Risks?		Price?

Motivation, vision and path are the three components to every transformation decision. If one component is missing or undeveloped, the decision will slow or not proceed at all. To the extent that any stakeholder in the decision doesn't share and support MVP, friction develops in the form of resistance to the decision.

Conversely, when you help potential clients recognize and assess risk, evaluate market threats and opportunities and envision a better alternative, you build trust and common purpose.

This, in turn, increases a prospect's motivation to make the transformation and reduces resistance to it. Transformation MVP explains *why* the decision to change is made. The transformation decision process explains *how* the decision to change is made.

The Three Stages of the Transformation Decision Process

Companies must continuously transform to realign themselves with changing market conditions to remain competitive. The more change in an industry, the more continuous the need to transform in order to remain competitive. The following diagram shows how a transformation decision progresses through three stages once a market change has been identified:

Transformation Decision Process

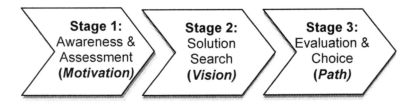

Market changes reach a point in *Stage 1: Motivation Stage* where the company begins to perceive a threat or opportunity. Assessment of the threat is initiated and, if the threat is considered significant enough, in *Stage 2: Vision Stage,* a search for a solution is undertaken. In *Stage 3: Path Stage* alternative solution paths are evaluated, and the company commits to a single course of action and executes its plan.

Once again, where Transformation MVP explains why transformation decisions are made, the Transformation Decision Process shows you how these decisions unfold, evolve and progress. Most often, the decision process (how) mirrors MVP (why). That is, a company generally discovers its motivation to leave current practices during Stage 1, seeks a new vision during Stage 2 and chooses a path to resolution and a service provider during Stage 3.

As you will see in subsequent chapters, determining both MVP and decision stage will be critical to your success in winning new business. These determinations will influence *what you recommend* and *when you recommend it.* For example, knowing why a prospect is interested in your service will guide what you recommend. Knowing how the prospect will make the decision and where they are in the decision-making process will help you know when to make your recommendations.

Let me give an example from a multinational company that recently committed to outsourced executive education. I interviewed the head of human resources, who told me she first became aware of the problem (*Stage 1: Motivation Stage*) when she received a call from the legal department saying the lack of general business knowledge was inhibiting the advancement of department staff. He wanted to know if HR offered any general business classes.

To assess the need for this type of education, HR conducted a survey of other departments and discovered that functional managers were not successfully making the adjustment to general management because their skills were "siloed," meaning the managers were limited by their functional perspective. The HR department then formed an executive committee to formalize the assessment and begin the search for remedies (*Stage 2: Vision Stage*).

At about this time a business development representative from a second-tier business school contacted the top HR manager, who agreed to meet knowing she may eventually need outside resources. The business development representative recognized that this potential client was still in *Stage 1: Motivation Stage* and moving toward *Stage 2: Vision Stage* of the transformation decision. The HR manager was not ready to choose a school, so the consultant offered diagnostic tools to help assess the need and provided market survey tools to help search for alternative business models.

Not wanting to create any obligation, the HR manager said she would welcome the support, but that any choice of outside vendors would be subject to a competitive bid process. The business development representative agreed to these terms recognizing this as an opportunity to establish a preferred provider position with a prospective client.

The assessment uncovered a broad management weakness that was clearly undermining effectiveness and growth (*Motivation*). The business development representative helped the committee survey outside organizations and determined that they needed to evolve into a more entrepreneurial organization (*Vision*). To accomplish that vision, the company would have to remove disincentives to entrepreneurial thinking and provide managers on an executive track with general business training (*Path to Resolution*).

Once the company decided that they did, in fact, need outside executive education resources to achieve the vision of becoming more entrepreneurial, they invited a select group of institutions to respond to a request for proposal (*Stage 3: Path Stage*). The second-tier institution that had supported the transformation decision was eventually chosen over the bigger-name alternatives despite intense lobbying from other senior executives and board members who either had attended the better-known institutions or wanted the prestige of being associated with them.

The HR manager took quite a professional risk in backing the second-tier institution. She did so because, "They understood what we were trying to do and demonstrated the capability, flexibility and commitment to see it through. The biggies were arrogant and clearly wanted us to do things their way."

As you can see, the choice of service provider was prompted by the broader transformation decision. Had the second-tier institution waited to engage the client until the company had entered the visible market with its RFP (*Stage 3: Path Stage*), it would have had little chance or prevailing against the more recognized alternatives.

Instead, the second-tier institution engaged the company while it was in one of the earlier stages of the transformation decision, helping them to recognize and define the problem(s) threatening their organization, envision and investigate alternatives and build preference for a specific path to resolution. By doing so, this service provider had already demonstrated value and established a level of familiarity and trust with the prospect.

When you engage a prospect early, your presence alone shines a light on the prospect's obstacles and offers the possibility of a solution. In addition, you can define the problem in the terms most favorable to what your firm can offer. Even if you don't win the business outright prior to an RFP, you have influenced the selection criteria in your favor.

Now, let's take a closer look at Motivation, Vision and Path as they will create the foundation for your invisible market strategy.

Motivation: *Evaluating the Need for Change*

Think back to a major change decision in your life, say a career change, marriage, divorce or relocation. How did it make your feel? Emotionally, most of us are uncomfortable with decisions involving change; we would prefer not to have to make them. The amount of stress associated with any such decision is a function of its importance (criticality), timing (urgency) and the uncertainty of its outcome (risk).

As executives, we have developed routines at work that we feel make us productive and competent at what we do. Methods and business habits become a well-worn path of business processes that give us a sense of comfort and control over our professional environment. Habits and routine mean we don't have to consciously choose anything. The illusion of predictability makes us feel safe in an unpredictable world.

In the corporate world, this inertia of current methods and practices is the result of an institutional need for balance. Complex organizations are assembled to reproduce standardized results. Standardized processes reduce costs and create competitive advantage. Most performance objectives are designed to build on previous objectives with ever increasing efficiency. The larger the organization, the more important it is that people and process are in balance.

Yet, this tendency to resist change can become the culprit in the eventual demise of a company. Companies that resist change too long become its victims as competitors who are more agile overtake them.

Given the natural resistance to change, it is surprising that transformation decisions occur at all. Clearly, motivation for change has to be compelling. Motivation, then, is both the driver and the prerequisite of change.

A key to success in the invisible market is to know how to uncover motivation, read it, increase it and harness it in a way that moves the prospect closer to a transformation decision. So where does that motivation come from?

The motivation for most business transformation decisions is a threatened performance objective. Performance objectives usually reflect the performance requirements of the company itself and those of each position within the firm.

Obstacles to Performance Objectives

When a market change occurs, it may create an obstacle to a performance objective and force us out of our comfort zone, leaving us feeling anxious and lost. As the perceived threat of continuing on the same path (status quo risk) increases, the motivation to find an alternative path increases.

The motivation for most business transformation decisions is a threatened performance objective. Individual business objectives usually reflect the performance requirements of the company and each position within the firm. The paramount business objectives are profitability and growth.

Objectives will change depending on the level, function and style of the decision maker. As you move down the organization's hierarchy, offspring objectives take on increasingly parochial attributes. For example, where the board and CEO are most occupied with shareholder value, growth and profitability, the CIO may be most concerned about equipment, integration, applications and user adoption. The chief marketing officer keeps an eye on revenue growth, pricing and market share. The chief manufacturing officer seeks to improve the quality of vendor inputs and reduce production costs and cycle times.

Take a minute and put yourself mentally and emotionally in your prospective client's shoes. What are your (the client's) performance objectives for this year? How will they be evaluated? By whom?

Performance objectives are themselves motivated by personal objectives, the most important of which are: prestige, power, pay and professional satisfaction.

Prestige has to do with recognition, reputation and image. How does this decision look to others in the client's company and to the outside world? How will it affect or threaten the prospect's status in the company or in the industry?

Power establishes position and authority within the organization and in the industry. How will this decision increase or decrease the decision-maker's authority or responsibility?

Pay encompasses all forms of extrinsic compensation. These include salary, stock and perks. Does a decision to use your company's services bode well for a prospect's personal wealth?

Professional satisfaction is the intrinsic compensation for the decision-maker. How will this decision improve your prospects satisfaction or sense of purpose?

When obstacles threaten your client's ability to meet his or her objectives – performance or personal – motivation for change builds and a search for solutions begins. Once again, return to the mind of your prospects.

What changes have occurred in your prospective client's company or market? What obstacles have those changes created that threaten client performance and personal objectives? What will happen if these obstacles are not addressed?

Predicting Transformation

Your biggest risk in the invisible market is wasting time with clients who can't or won't make a transformation decision. If you can read your prospect's motivation, you can make better use of your limited time and resources.

Just because a company has a problem that you can address does not mean that company is prepared to make a transformation decision. Companies are faced with hundreds of problems. However, only those perceived as *critical* and *urgent* reach the necessary threshold of motivation. The **Change Motivation Scale** below shows the various levels of motivation and potential for change.

Change Motivation Scale

Obstacle Criticality	Urgency Indications	Change Potential
Unknown or resolved	No interest	Dormant
Nuisance	Attention, low priority, low urgency	Latent
Problem	Assessment but no schedule	Possible
Threat	Action commitment, deadline set	Probable
Crisis	Taking action, urgent deadline	Certain

Think about a few of the prospects you are working with now. Locate their motivation on the change motivation scale. What is the likelihood that they will actually make a transformation decision? In Chapter 6, we'll talk about how to align your sales strategy according to where prospects are on this chart.

Vision: A Better Place to Go

Even motivated prospects won't make a transformation decision unless a better alternative is visible and attainable. In our previous example, the company was aware that managers stuck in functional silos were threatening its productivity and growth. But that company's HR department needed to identify, define and build consensus for its vision of becoming a more entrepreneurial company before it could act decisively.

Problems are not actionable until they have been linked to a clear vision of a better future. Vision becomes more compelling with clarity, consensus and certainty of outcome. Clarity adds definition; consensus creates ownership; and certainty reduces risk. If you have ever built or remodeled a house or garden, think about how much easier your decision to move forward became when you saw the drawings. Similarly, career dissatisfaction does not lead to a job change until you see another available job or career path that offers a better future.

When sufficient motivation to change is bolstered by a shared vision of an improved future for the organization, this unifies purpose; such strength of purpose makes the pain (effort, cost, disruption and risk) of transformation tolerable. When a potential client possesses both purpose and ability to act, the prospect is then ready for transformation.

Are you able to help potential clients envision a better future? How can you help them see and buy into that vision? How can you build confidence that the vision can be achieved? The more a prospect can see, feel and believe in the alternative vision, the easier it is for them to let go of the status quo.

Path to Resolution:
The Way to Reach the Vision Destination

Finally, a transformation decision will not occur until an organization has a clear and reliable path to achieve its vision.

This path to resolution must be within the prospect's means. What good is an unachievable vision alternative?

The path to resolution is where prospects will encounter the most pain during the transformation process. Solutions take effort, cost money, cause disruption and carry risks; these things cause pain. If the pain (i.e., effort, cost, disruption, or risk) of your path is perceived to be greater than status quo risk and the attraction of the vision, the prospect will resist your solution.

Clarity and consensus make visions more attractive, but lack of awareness, lack of understanding and bias will add resistance. The prospect company may not be aware that a solution is available. They may not understand that your solution or your vision is distinctive from current or previously tried remedies.

Previous failures or successes may also bias an executive against making what he perceives as another risky decision. Emotional resistance can be caused by lack of confidence, commitment and trust in the service provider. The executive you are dealing with may be unsure about whether you will be capable of and committed to doing what you say you can do.

Because of this risk exposure, companies compare various service providers. This competition, which occurs at the path to resolution stage of the transformation decision, includes the evaluation of various vendors by the prospect and a choice among alternative service providers.

During this phase, organizations begin to make the service provider decision; that is, choosing the service provider who can best help them with their transformation decision. It is at this point that the prospect enters the visible market.

Transformation Value: *Purpose Minus Pain*

So far, we have seen that transformation decisions are motivated by market changes that create status quo risk. They gain momentum as alternative visions become clear and attractive. To proceed, they require a reliable path to deliver the client from status quo risk to vision reward. That path will usually require the help of a professional service provider.

The decision to proceed with a transformation reaches critical mass when purpose becomes greater than pain. In other words, prospects will act when a motivating threat and an attractive vision outweigh the pain (effort, cost, disruption and risk) of the proposed path. Therefore, your role as a service provider supporting the transformation decision is to increase motivation and vision attraction and decrease the pain of your path toward a solution.

Armed with a deeper understanding of transformational MVP and the decision process, we will use this strategic empathy to build your strategy to penetrate, build value and win clients in the invisible market.

Chapter 2:
Glossary of Terms and Key Concepts

Transformation Decision - A decision to abandon current practices in favor of a new approach. This requires a commitment to a new strategy, process, team or resource allocation. Before they hire you, potential clients make two decisions: 1) they decide to transform some part of their business (transformation decision), and 2) they choose your firm among a field of competitors to help them make the desired change (service provider decision). A transformation decision leads to and is a prerequisite for the service provider decision. Transformation decisions generally occur in the invisible market.

Transformation MVP - Transformation decisions have three critical components: a *motivation* to leave current practices, a clear *vision* of a better future state and a reliable *path* to attain the vision and resolve the problem. Motivation, vision and path are the three components to every transformation decision. If one is missing or undeveloped, the decision will slow or not proceed.

Three Stages of the Transformation Decision Process -
- *Stage 1: Motivation Stage* - The company becomes aware of a threat (or opportunity). Assessment of the threat is initiated; if the threat is considered significant enough, a search for alternatives begins.
- *Stage 2: Vision Stage* - The company envisions and searches for possible solutions to obstacles uncovered in Stage 1.
- *Stage 3: Path Stage* - Alternative solution paths are evaluated, and the company commits to one and takes action.

Motivation - A critical and/or urgent reason to leave current practices usually caused by marketplace changes that threaten performance or personal objectives. Motivation is both the driver and the prerequisite of change. As the perceived threat of continuing on the same path (status quo risk) increases, so does the motivation to find an alternative path. Only threats and crises are likely to lead to transformation decisions.

Vision - Vision is the expected and preferred outcome or destination of change. Vision becomes more compelling with clarity, consensus and certainty of outcome. Clarity adds definition; consensus creates ownership; and certainty reduces risk. Even motivated prospects won't make a transformation decision unless a better alternative is visible and attainable. When sufficient motivation to change is bolstered by a shared vision of an improved future for the organization, this unifies purpose; such strength of purpose makes the pain (effort, cost, disruption and risk) of transformation more tolerable.

Path to Resolution - A company's clear and reliable way to achieve its vision within its means. The path to resolution is where prospects will encounter the most pain during the transformation process. Solutions take effort, cost money, cause disruption and carry risks; these things cause pain. If such sources of pain are perceived by the prospect to be greater than the risks of maintaining the status quo, the prospect will resist your solution.

Transformation Value - Transformation value equals purpose minus pain. A transformation will advance when purpose exceeds pain. Prospects will act when a motivating threat and an attractive vision outweigh the pain (effort, cost, disruption and risk) of the proposed path. Therefore, your role as a service provider is to increase motivation and vision attraction and decrease the pain of your path toward a solution.

Chapter 3

Value Mining:
Aligning Your Strategy
to the Prospect's MVP

To establish preferred or sole provider status in the invisible market successful service sellers use a strategy that I call **Value Mining**. Value mining is the process of finding a potential client's perception of value and decision stage and then aligning to that perception and stage.

Value Mining bridges **value gaps** that cause decision friction and leads to faster and more comfortable decisions in your favor. Specifically, value mining involves: 1) identifying and accessing high potential clients, 2) finding and influencing their MVP, and then 3) aligning your recommendations to support the prospect's MVP and decision process.

In my research, I found that successful service providers were more likely to align their sales strategy to be in sync with the prospect's transformation MVP and decision process. This is a strategy that I call **Value Mining**, and it looks like this:

Client Transformation Decision Process
(*What the Client Is Doing*)

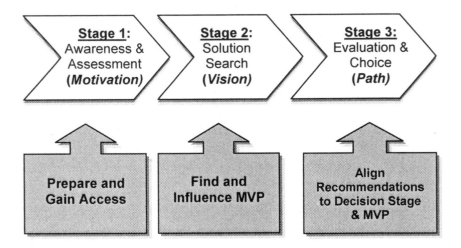

Your Value Mining Strategy

Successful service providers entering the invisible market determine which prospects are willing and able to make a transformation decision and then focus their resources on those qualified opportunities. This is typically accomplished through face-to-face meetings. So the first step in value mining is to identify and gain access to high potential prospects.

Once in front of the prospect, successful service providers support the transformation decision by finding and influencing the prospect's MVP. They find and influence motivation by identifying and exploring the consequences of problems and threats. If the prospect is already motivated, they then help the qualified prospect to envision and build consensus for solution alternatives. They also attempt to uncover and address potential resistance early.

Finally, they make appropriate recommendations aligned with the prospect's MVP and decision stage. Successful service providers ensure that their recommendations advance the prospect's decision while also building preference for their firm's services over others. That sounds straightforward but is quite challenging in light of the inevitable value gaps that service providers face along the way.

As we discussed earlier, potential clients in the invisible market are either in the process of making a transformation decision or are dormant. If they are dormant, they have no reason to meet with you. If they are in the early stages of making a transformation decision, they may not yet be ready to meet with you. In fact, the prospective client in the invisible market may resist you at *every* step of the value mining process; they may resist meeting, sharing problems, exploring solutions or choosing you over alternatives.

Value Mining Points of Resistance

Let's explore why potential clients may resist meeting, sharing their problems, exploring solutions or committing to you. These resistance points are caused by **value gaps**. By analyzing these value gaps, you can improve your strategic empathy and create appropriate responses. The following analysis suggests reasons potential clients may resist your value mining efforts:

Resistance Analysis

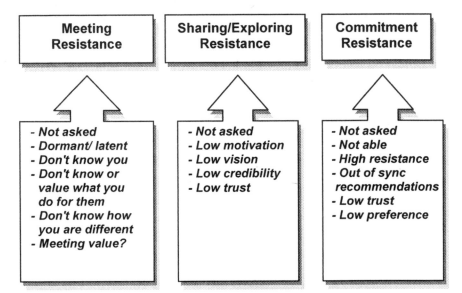

Meeting Resistance	Sharing/Exploring Resistance	Commitment Resistance
- Not asked - Dormant/ latent - Don't know you - Don't know or value what you do for them - Don't know how you are different - Meeting value?	- Not asked - Low motivation - Low vision - Low credibility - Low trust	- Not asked - Not able - High resistance - Out of sync recommendations - Low trust - Low preference

Resistance to a Face-to-Face Meeting

Why won't prospects meet with you? Clearly, potential clients will not meet with you unless they are asked. I have included this as a resistance point, but it is obviously self-inflicted. Professional service providers tend to significantly underestimate the number of face-to-face calls necessary to succeed in the invisible market. In fact, this is the biggest cause of failure.

When it comes to meetings, doing it often is even more important than doing it well – but doing it well certainly helps. Your reluctance to make calls or to ask directly for meetings is understandable; no one likes to face rejection or to feel undervalued and unappreciated. Certainly, busy prospects may not welcome your calls or queries with open arms.

But keep in mind that prospects may not be rejecting you outright; rather, they may be communicating that their motivation level is too low at this time. This provides you with information you needed to know anyway. So, a rebuffed meeting could save you hours of precious time. If you're able to learn that the prospect's motivation hasn't yet reached critical mass, you've gained insight into the prospect's MVP.

On the other hand, you may suspect that a potential client *does* need your help but just does not realize it yet. In that case, the rebuffed meeting presents a value gap for both of you. Resistance arises because the prospect does not know you, does not realize that you can help or does not realize that you offer something different than what they have seen or done previously. In this case, the prospect does not yet see the value of a meeting with you or your firm.

Sharing and Exploring Resistance

Why won't potential clients share their problems or explore your solutions? When service providers offer solutions before prospective clients are motivated to change, it is called Premature Solution Syndrome. This is a common problem for vendor-centric experts who see the prospect's problem and solution before the prospect does. Remember that value equals purpose minus pain. By presenting a path (i.e. the pain) before purpose is established, you undermine the value of your solution. We'll talk more about how to avoid the Premature Solution Syndrome in Chapter 5.

Finding and influencing MVP is the core of the Value Mining Process. If the prospect will not share problems or explore solutions, you cannot determine or align to their MVP (motivation, vision and path). Once again, sharing and exploring resistance may be self-inflicted. Frequently, service providers are so busy showing off their expertise that they neglect to ask questions of the prospect. Resistance to sharing could also be caused by other factors including low motivation, low trust or because they don't feel that you can help them.

Resistance to Commitment

Why won't potential clients commit to your solution? Once you have determined your prospect's Transformation MVP, the next step in the process is to align your strategy, message and service to gain agreement and commitment to your solution. Prospective clients will resist your efforts if their motivation is low, if the vision lacks clarity and consensus or if they perceive the price, disruption or risk is too high.

Resistance to commitment can also be caused by recommendations that are out of sync with the potential client's decision process. Once the transformation decision is made, possible reasons a prospect may not select your firm include: your failure to ask for a commitment, the prospect's inability to act, the prospect's preference for a competitive service provider or a prospect's corporate policy which requires opening all vendor choices to competition.

Bridging the Value Gap

In the remainder of the book, you will see and practice tactics used by successful service providers to bridge these value gaps. If you listen carefully to what prospects are communicating and respond accordingly, you can systematically bridge each value gap or appropriately withdraw.

As you learn more about Value Mining and its stages in the coming chapters, you will become skilled in gaining agreement from prospects—in effect, at gaining their permission – to move forward through each stage. This will eliminate wasting time with prospects who aren't ready for your solution and will help you focus on those who are.

To overcome meeting resistance, in Chapter 4 you will reengineer your value proposition. Instead of comparing yourself to alternatives, you will realign your "go-to-market" message to support transformation MVP. To encourage your invisible market prospects to share problems and explore solutions, in Chapters 5, 6 and 7 you will construct and execute a questioning strategy that encourages collaboration and builds MVP.

To prepare your prospect and yourself for your proposal, in Chapters 8 and 9 you will align your solution to each prospect's MVP, situation and decision-making process. Finally, if and when the prospect invites a competitive comparison, in Chapters 10, 11 and 12 you will see why and how this comparison is made, and be able to align your message and strategy to build preference over competitors.

The first step in Value Mining is to gain access to the prospective clients by re-engineering your value proposition so that your capabilities align with their anticipated transformation MVP. We'll look at how to do that in the next chapter.

Chapter 3:
Glossary of Terms and Key Concepts

Value Mining - Value mining is the process of finding and then aligning to a potential client's perception of value and decision stage. Value mining bridges value gaps that cause decision friction and leads to faster and more comfortable decisions made in your favor. Specifically, it involves: 1) identifying and accessing high potential clients, 2) finding and influencing MVP, and then 3) aligning your recommendations to support MVP and the decision process.

Value Mining Resistance Points - Value gaps may cause a prospective client to resist you at every step of the value mining process. They may resist scheduling meetings, sharing problems, exploring solutions or choosing you over alternatives.

Meeting Resistance - Clients may resist meeting with you because they don't perceive a problem, they don't know you, they don't know what you can do for them or they don't understand how you are different. Perhaps the biggest reason they don't meet with you is because they have not been asked.

Sharing/Exploring Resistance - Prospective clients will not be inclined to share their problems and explore your solutions if they are not asked or are not motivated. They will also not share or explore such issues if they don't trust you or don't believe that you can help them.

Commitment Resistance - Clients may not commit to you if they are not asked or if they prefer a competitor. They will not commit to you if they are not able or not willing or if your recommendation is out of sync with their MVP or stage of decision.

Chapter 4

Gain Access to the Invisible Market:
Charting Your MVP Value Proposition

Invisible Market Strategy

Y our current value proposition may work well
in the visible market where prospective clients compare and choose from among alternative providers. However, your existing value
proposition may not be relevant to those prospects who have not yet made the transformation
decision. The most successful business professionals develop a clear message to reach this
"invisible market."

In this chapter you see how to re-engineer
your "go to market" value proposition by aligning
it to anticipated MVP (Motivation, Vision and
Path to Resolution) using a tool called a MVP
Value Chart. This chart will be used in later
chapters to develop an MVP Questioning Strategy and an MVP Presentation Strategy. Value
charting will help you understand and articulate
your value in the invisible market and provide
answers to the first question potential new

clients ask before agreeing to meet with you –
"What can you do for me?"

Identify Your Service Value Proposition
What is the value of the service that you provide?

Notice that I am not asking you why you are better than a competitor? I am asking why a potential new client should be interested in the services that you or your competitors offer? This is what I refer to as service value. Interestingly, most of the professionals I work with initially find it difficult to articulate their service value. They can describe what they do, who they do it for and even why it works, but why it is valuable? Well, that's a bit more challenging.

In the invisible market, prospective clients are not yet interested in how you compare to other service providers. They need to know why they should care about the service you provide at all. They don't need the service provider if they don't see the value of the service.

At a recent client meeting, I asked the assembled professionals to define their **service value proposition**. Some of their answers were typical—value is in our expertise, value is price, value is in our process, value is what the client gets, and so on.

One of my favorite answers was that value included benefits that the client knew they would receive *and* benefits they were unaware of before the start of the engagement. When I heard that one, I asked, "How much was the client willing to pay for the value they didn't know about when the engagement contract was signed?" The answer, of course, was nothing.

This is another example of a value gap – the difference between the client's perception of value before the engagement and the actual value you can deliver. Your service value proposition is your first opportunity to connect and align with a prospect. If you can establish a beachhead of value, prospective clients will be more inclined to see you initially, use your services, choose you over alternatives and pay what you're worth. For that to happen, the prospective client must quickly recognize what you can do for him or her.

Each potential client has a unique perception of value that can only be uncovered in face-to-face communications. However, to gain access to prospects in the invisible market, you will need to build and be able to articulate a "go-to-market" value proposition that anticipates the motivation and resistance that you will find there. Your "go-to-market" value proposition is based on your previous client experience, knowledge of the prospect's industry and advance research that you do on the prospect.

What Can You Do... *for Me?*

Is your value proposition vendor- or client-centric?

Value propositions that *only* answer the question "What do you do?" are **vendor-centric**. A vendor-centric message is built on the premise that the more prospective clients know about you, the more likely they will be to choose you. It leaves it to your prospects to answer, "What does that mean to me?" A vendor-centric message creates a value gap by leaving unanswered the critical *"for me?"* part of the prospect's question, as shown below.

Vendor-Centric Message
What Can You Do?   *For Me?*

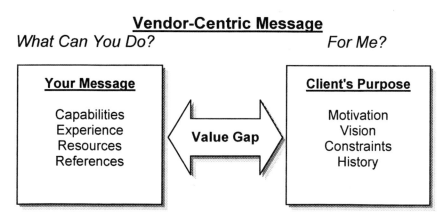

A vendor-centric message might establish your expertise and get you invited to an RFP, but it may not build value in the invisible market because it does not connect your expertise with the prospect's needs. It doesn't build a transformation partnership.

"How the hell is he going to help me? He's dead!"

If your service value proposition is vendor-centric, you might be surprised to hear what prospects are thinking about your message. My interviews with service buyers revealed a consistent frustration with irrelevant vendor-centric presentations.

As an executive responsible for running a major hotel chain, Arthur "Bud" Barrett hired hundreds of service providers. Barrett is representative of many service buyers; here is what he had to say about the countless vendor-centric sales presentations he has witnessed over the years:

"They come in and put on a song and dance about how great they are, how long they have been in business and how many offices they have around the world," Barrett said. "I had no idea why they thought this was important. It was just part of the ritual. One group even put up a picture of the founder of the firm and I'm thinking, 'How the hell is he going to help me? He's dead!'"

In the invisible market, prospective clients don't really care what you do, what you have done, who you have done it for, how many offices you have, how many years you have been in business, or even that you are a "total solutions provider." They only want to know *what you can do for them*. Your capabilities and resources are only valuable when the executives to whom you are selling perceive that those capabilities and resources may help them solve their problems or achieve their objectives – in other words, when your services fit their purposes.

Unlike the vendor-centric message, the **client-centric message** bridges the value gap by answering the "What can you do for me?" question, which naturally dominates a prospective client's thinking. A client-centric message is built on the assumption that the more you know about your prospect, the easier it is to build value and help them. As previously discussed, a prospective client's perception of your value becomes more positive as he or she sees that you and your services are rationally and emotionally aligned with his or her purpose and path.

To answer the "for me" part of the prospect's question, link your capabilities to the client's motivation and vision. This is accomplished in three simple steps:

1) **Identify** which problems your services address,
2) **Articulate** a clear vision of a better future for the prospect, that you can help the prospect achieve
3) **Demonstrate** how (only) your service and expertise will help them realize their vision.

Let me give you a real-life example. One of my clients was an executive search firm. Their vendor-centric sales message highlighted their large database, screening tools and 25 years in business. Meanwhile, their prospective clients were worried that unfilled key positions or weak placements were preventing them from executing their business plan. The search firm had impressive service capabilities but left it to potential clients to find value in those capabilities. That left a value gap.

Enough about Me

To help this firm find its value, I guided them through an exercise I call **MVP Value Charting**. Here is how we charted the original message:

Value Gap

What Can You Do?   *For Me?*

Search Firm Capabilities	**Value Gap** What does that *for me?*	**Client Motivation & Vision**
- Large database - Screening tools - 25 years		- Execute Business Plan - Hire best people

"What Does That Do for Me?"

The best way to extract the relevance (value) of your service and close the value gap is to examine each of your service capabilities and ask "What does that do for the prospective client?" or "So what?" until you reach the prospect's motivation or vision. I call these *vision links* because they create a path from your service to the client's vision.

A client-centric message might look like this:

Vision Links

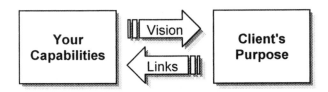

The Client-Centric Message

Returning to the search firm example, here's how we discovered and charted the vision links related to the firm's large database:

"We offer an extensive database of qualified candidates."
What does a database do for the client?
–"It gives the client access to a large candidate pool."
What does that do for the client?
–"That gives the client more choice."
What does that do for the client?
–"The client is more likely to find the best candidate."
What does that do for the client?
–"The right candidate can help the client better execute his strategy. At this level the right candidate can be the difference between success and failure for the company."
"What else does the database do for clients?" (I asked

this question since the same service will frequently enable multiple objectives.)
—"It gives them faster access to qualified candidates."
So what?
—"They can fill positions faster."
So what?
—"A missing key player can slow strategy execution, which is threatening to the organization. By filling the position faster, the client can move ahead with their strategy sooner."

The Client-Centric Message

What Can You Do?   *For Me?*

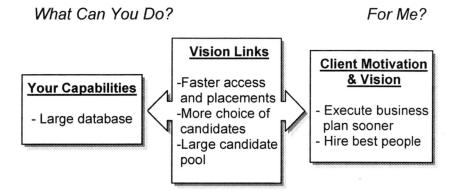

The vision links of *faster access* and *faster placements* build a path to the vision of executing the strategy sooner. The vision links of *choice* and *larger candidate pool* create a path to the vision of *hiring the best people.*

This is a simplified version of a more complex MVP value charting exercise I work through with my clients. A more complete version of the value chart includes more about the prospective client's motivation, vision and path and looks like this.

Search Firm MVP Value Chart

Motivation or Status Quo Risk	Vision Objective	Vision Link "So What?"	Service Capability	Proof
Weak executives create drag on growth	Hire best people	- More choice of candidates - Larger candidate pool	Extensive database	References, highest client satisfaction in survey
Unfilled key position hurting our performance	Execute strategy sooner	- Fill position sooner - Faster access to candidates	Extensive database	35,000 executives in database
Don't want to waste time with candidates who don't fit our culture	Hire best fit	- Only interview good fits - Screens out misfits	Candidate screening tools	25 percent faster placement on average
Don't have the time or access to do it myself	Better use of my time	-We can handle it for you -Proven process	25 years in business	75 percent reduction in placement turnover

As you can see, the **MVP Value Chart** has five columns, beginning with the client's problem and working backward to your services, following the natural progression of the manner in which prospective clients will value you and your services. An explanation of each column and its contents follows:

• **Motivation/Status Quo Risk** includes the obstacles to personal and performance objectives and their long-term consequences that motivate the transformation decision. We plugged in the search firm's prospective client's motivation, that is, the problem(s) the firm could fix for the prospect. In this case, the search firm anticipated that their prospect would be concerned about how unfilled positions threaten strategy, how weak people create a drag on growth, how poor candidates waste time, or how the firm's executives do not have time to conduct the search.

• **Vision Objectives** convert obstacles to actionable objectives that give you and your prospective client a shared vision of the future. As we saw in the earlier explanation of transformation decisions, problems can motivate transformation only if there is a compelling alternative vision. A company is unlikely to abandon current practices (i.e. the status quo) without clear view of a better future state. In this MVP Value Chart, the search firm converted problem statements into a shared vision that then becomes the foundation for a successful service partnership.

• **Vision Links** help prospects overcome problems and realize visions. They also connect your service capabilities with a client's motivation and vision. Here, the search firm answered the critical "So what?" question, joining their firm's capabilities with the vision objectives of their prospective client.

• **Service Capabilities** are the resources, experiences, processes and tools used to affect change. These are the initial and vendor-centric sales messages that search firm had previously used.

• **Proof** gives the prospective client evidence of your capabilities, provides confidence in you and your services and/or reduces resistance to your solution(s). So far, our efforts to align vendor-client value have dealt with both sides of the service value equation. We've increased motivation for change by identifying problems, and we have offered a vision of a better future. We've reduced resistance to change by providing a clear and logical path to resolution with service capabilities and vision links.

But the prospective client is still faced with a significant concern: "How do I know it will work for me?" To build maximum value, you need to reduce the threat that it might not work by providing proof of your reliability. What quantifiable evidence can you present that adds reliability to your solution outcome?

How would you reduce the perception of effort, disruption or cost?

In the executive search firm's example, evidence of *faster completed searches, more choices, higher client satisfaction,* or *better results* would go a long way to reduce the perception of risk, effort and disruption. Their completed MVP Value Chart includes concrete performance proof such as *independent rankings, database characteristics,* or *speed and success statistics.*

Create Your Own MVP Value Chart

Think of your service in the MVP context. What are the problems that you solve? How do your clients express their concerns? How would your clients express their vision objectives? How do clients perceive the effort, disruption, cost and risk of your visions? How would you minimize those pain perceptions?

Create your own MVP Value Chart – even if you begin by jotting down a few notes on the back of a napkin. Creating a chart will help you to better see and express your value to clients. Later in this book, we will use your Value Chart to create both a questioning strategy and a proposal presentation.

To complete your own client-centric MVP Value Chart, follow these steps:

1) What are the top three motivators (problems, causes and threats) that you can help your potential client address? What are the longer-term consequences of these obstacles? Plug them into the **"Motivation"** section.

2) What better future can you help your prospective client achieve? Convert problems into client **"Vision Objectives"** and put them into the "Vision/ Objective" box.

3) Plug in the **"Service Capabilities"** that address those problems.

4) Add the **"Vision Links"** by starting with your Service Capability. Then ask, "So what?" until you have reached the client vision or motivation. (There may be more than one vision link.)

5) What anecdotes, statistics, third-party evaluations or rankings, validations, or client statements can you offer as evidence to support your claims and add comfort to the client? Plug these into the **"Proof"** column.

Your ability to clearly answer the client's overriding question ("What can you do for me?") is critical to your ability to gain access to targeted executives. Once you complete your own MVP Value Chart, you will have a clear indication of how to present your service value proposition in a succinct manner.

Emotional Alignment

Of course, gaining access to the invisible market isn't just about what you have to say. Your message gives a prospect a rational reason to see you, but it is familiarity that bridges the **emotional value gap**.

Think about the professional services you have purchased yourself. Who is your lawyer, accountant, money manager, doctor, estate planner, or other service provider? Did you conduct an exhaustive search and ask for a request for proposal? Probably not.

When we need a service provider, we typically start with the familiar and then work our way out. We ask: Can I do it? Can someone I know do it? Do I know someone who knows some one who can do it?

Familiarity is, in fact, the single most important consideration when choosing a service provider. The reason we choose people close to us to provide key services is that we trust them more. We want to choose people who are emotionally aligned with us because they understand our motivation, share our vision and are often personally committed to helping us reach that vision. Although you would not retain a good friend if that person were not qualified, the people you know and trust have a distinct advantage over even those with potentially stronger capabilities.

So start your networking from the familiar and then work your way out. Begin with existing clients and friends. Who do they know? To whom might they introduce or refer you? Try to make each contact produce two additional contacts. You may find that you can work your way into the invisible market without making a single cold call.

Once you gain access to the market, your next step is to prepare for face-to-face meetings where you will want clients to share problems and explore solutions. Your **MVP Value Chart** will become the foundation of the **MVP Questioning Strategy** that we'll discuss in the next chapter.

Chapter 4:
Glossary of Terms and Key Concepts

Service Value - Service value is the perception of worth or need a prospective client may have for the services that you and your competitors provide.

Vendor-centric Value Proposition - A vendor-centric value proposition highlights your expertise and capabilities but is silent on client motivation and vision. It is built on the premise that the more prospective clients know about you, the more likely they will be to choose you. It leaves it to your prospects to answer, "What does that mean to me?" Although a vendor-centric message can get you invited and help you establish credibility, it creates a value gap by leaving it to the prospect to connect the vendor capabilities to its needs and situation.

Client-centric Value Proposition - A client-centric value proposition focuses on the prospective client's likely motivation and vision. It is built on the assumption that the more you know about your prospect, the easier it is to connect to your prospect's perception of value. A prospective client's perception of your value increases as they see that you are rationally and emotionally aligned with their purpose and path.

Service Value Charting - Service value charting is a method of converting vendor-centric value propositions into client centric value propositions by asking "So What?" until you have created *vision links* from your service capabilities to your composite client's motivation and vision.

Vision Links - Vision links help prospects overcome problems, realize visions and connect your service capabilities with their motivation and vision.

Chapter 5

Face-to-Face Value Mining:
Shaping an MVP Questioning Strategy

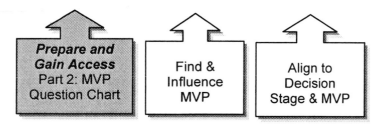

S ervice providers tend to offer their solutions before they or the prospects are ready for them. That makes their proposals less valuable and therefore less likely to reach a successful conclusion.

This chapter shows you how to "present" your value with questions using an **MVP Questioning Strategy** that converts your MVP Value Chart into key questions that not only demonstrate your capabilities but also: 1) encourage prospects to share critical information, 2) build their perception of need, 3) reveal their likelihood for change, and 4) locate the prospect in the decision-making process.

One of the biggest mistakes service providers make in the invisible market is offering solutions prematurely. I discovered this both in my research and from personal experience.

Just the other night at a party, a friend of mine, a senior executive at a large construction company, told me that a fall-off in business was forcing his people to work harder to dig up new business. I immediately suggested a sales training workshop. But as soon as it came out of my mouth, I knew I had made a fatal error. Even after years of practice, I had made the same common mistake I continually warn my clients about.

This is a mistake I call the **Premature Solution Syndrome** – offering a solution before the prospect is motivated to resolve a problem *and* before the service provider fully understands the prospect's situation. Just as most service professionals do, I saw my friend's problem and its solution before he did. But my solution lacked value because he was not yet motivated to make a transformation decision.

A better approach would have been to use a value mining strategy to find and build value so that both my prospective client and I would have been better prepared for a recommendation or proposal. Using the value mining strategy I would have suggested a meeting where we could have identified and assessed the problem and then explored the long-term consequences if things remained unresolved.

If the problem had been critical and urgent, the next step would have been to establish actionable objectives and begin to frame a solution vision. To clear the way for a recommendation, I would have found out what the company was doing now, what had been done in the past, how these actions had worked, who had made decisions and how those decisions had been reached.

Because I neglected to value mine this opportunity my recommendation lacked value. My construction friend politely commented that a workshop might be a good idea, and that ended the conversation. Once I had made the recommendation, it would have been pushy to go back and try to establish a better value foundation.

As a service provider, you've spent years perfecting your craft. Oddly enough, that expertise can actually work to your disadvantage when acquiring new clients, or winning follow-up business from existing clients, because it can put you out of sync with your prospect's transformation decision. Just because *you* know a potential client has a problem doesn't mean that *he or she* knows it. And until they do recognize the danger of continuing to do things in the same way, you will encounter value gap resistance.

One Client at a Time

You don't sell a standardized product and you don't sell to a mass market. Each prospect has different objectives, obstacles, personality, decision process, resources, experiences and deadlines. If you are going to be their partner, prospects want you to understand their unique circumstances; they want you to be personally invested in their objectives. Your knowledge of the client and his or her particular situation demonstrates commitment and builds comfort and trust.

Unfortunately, many service providers still treat their service and their potential clients alike. They "customize" their PowerPoint slides by adding prospect logos to their "boilerplate" vendor-centric presentations and then wonder why they lose on price. They try to fit the market to the message.

In the invisible market, the only way to determine the prospect's motivation and vision is through face-to-face communication. This is where things can get complicated. The dilemma of a new relationship is that both buyer and seller need more information for the relationship to become relevant and worthwhile, as the following graphic demonstrates.

Sales Communication Complexity

What the prospect needs to know about you to close value gaps:	What you need to know to support the transformation decision:
Rational: Understanding • Who are you? • What do you do? • How are you different? • Is there a good reason to talk, listen, and share with you? Emotional: Trust Are you: • Credible? • Capable? • Committed to me? • Likable? • Focused on my situation and me?	Motivation: Is the prospect motivated to change? Vision: Do they know where they are going? Path: Have they committed to a solution? Ability: Does the prospect have: • Authority? • Consensus? • Budget? Preference: Does the prospect: • Understand my difference? • Value my difference?

You need to know the prospect's motivation (M), vision (V) and point along the path toward resolution (P) so you can support the transformation decision and align your recommendation to the prospect's MVP. The prospect needs to know if you are capable and trustworthy before they will give you the information you need. They also need to see that you offer something different than similar service providers.

At this juncture, if you choose to use a vendor-centric approach and do all the talking, then you won't establish the strategic empathy needed to close the value gap. The prospect will learn about your capabilities but may not see how those capabilities help her, won't know if you understand her present situation and won't know if you are trustworthy.

Bridging the value gap requires a method of communicating with prospects that is both client-centric *and* interactive. Therefore, you need a questioning strategy that allows you to express and acquire key points of both emotional and rational communication. That builds a foundation for an engagement partnership.

The Expert and the Listener

A few years ago I had a personal experience that shows with great clarity the difference between a vendor-centric presentation approach and client-centric questioning approach to business development.

When a close friend died leaving a wife and two children, I knew it was time to stop putting off my own estate planning. Viewed as a transformation decision, my motivation to protect my family increased with the death of my friend. I was in the search and assessment of alternatives phase of transformation because I did not have a clear vision or plan yet. Ironically, however, it was my first discussion with an estate planner that caused me to delay taking action despite my newly found motivation.

The first estate planner, let's call him "the Expert," knew his stuff. He went on and on about living wills, irrevocable trusts, tax implications, generation skipping and probate. He even gave me a copy of his book to read before we continued.

He convinced me of his expertise, but he also made me feel that I needed to learn more before I could make these important decisions. Instead of helping me clarify my vision and begin developing a plan, he raised my resistance. So instead of proceeding, I promised myself I would read up a bit more before making any decisions. Months went by without much progress.

Things probably would have stayed that way but for a chance meeting. At my son's soccer game, I discovered that one of the other parents was an estate planner; we'll call her "the Listener." You'll see why in a minute.

At half time I decided to catch up on my estate planning homework and asked the Listener a question about irrevocable trusts. Instead of answering she asked me what I was trying to accomplish. I said I was worried that estate taxes would leave my family with too little to maintain our standard of living. She then proceeded to explain in layman's terms how I could financially protect my family by transferring wealth to my children using an irrevocable trust.

She asked me a few more questions. She told me how I could save my family the pain of difficult decisions with a living will, how to direct the care of my children if both my wife and I died, and how to keep my kids from inheriting too much wealth at once all with a clarity that seemed to make the decisions much easier.

As the boys came back on the field, she said, "Bob, if you are interested in setting up a legal and financial plan to protect your family, we can do it in three short meetings. In the first I will ask you questions to determine your situation and objectives (Value Mining). In the second I will show you how we can accomplish your objectives with the various planning tools (value aligning), and in the last we will sign and notarize your estate plan (converting value into action)." Two weeks later it was done.

What made the difference? I was highly motivated to hire an estate planner from the start, but the Expert's vendor-centric message failed to build value with me. He was eloquent in describing what he could do, but left it to me to figure out how his knowledge would help me reach my objective of protecting my family. I respected the Expert and was impressed by what he knew, but I was not inclined to form a partnership with him. That left a value gap.

In comparison, the Listener focused on my needs rather

than on impressing me with her expertise. Her approach was client-centric. Her questions demonstrated her expertise while also making me feel she understood my situation. She helped me find value by clarifying what I wanted (my vision), aligned to my value by positioning her capabilities in the context of my vision objectives, and then presented a clear path to resolution. In short, she aligned her capabilities with my motivation and a shared vision to create a plan and a partnership. That client-centric approach eliminated the value gap and made my decision easy.

Questioning Vs. Pitching

Without exception, the successful business developers I interviewed emphasized the importance of questioning and listening over presenting in their communications with prospects. The executives who retain service providers told me time and again that they learn more about service providers' capabilities through the questions that service providers asked than through their sales presentations.

The service providers who asked questions and listened also built deeper emotional connection and started to create strategic empathy. As one corporate counsel who purchased over $14 million annually in outside legal services told me, "I listen to how well they are listening to me."

So, if your ability to ask insightful questions is considered important by service buyers and you need to obtain critical information from prospects to be able to close the value gap, it makes sense to use a communication style that involves a questioning strategy rather than one in which you talk and the prospect listens. Such a questioning strategy has several key benefits. It –

- helps the prospect experience your expertise
- encourages a prospect to share critical information
- helps the prospect recognize threats and solutions on his or her own
- reveals the prospects likelihood for change
- helps determine where a prospect is in the transformation decision process

Building an MVP Question Strategy

OK so questioning and listening are better than pitching. Almost any sales book or seminar in the last 50 years would have told you that. But why do most service providers still do all of the talking? In my experience it is because service providers practice presentations, but they don't practice a questioning strategy. They frequently are not sure what questions to ask and when and how they should be asked. To help you develop and practice your questioning strategy try converting your presentation into an interactive discussion.

You used a MVP value chart to build a "go to market" message. Now let's use that same value chart to create an MVP questioning strategy that demonstrates your capabilities, that helps you gather critical information and that helps the prospect recognize threats and opportunities. This MVP Question Chart begins like this:

MVP Question Chart

Motivation	Vision Objective	Vision Link	Resistance
1. Problem? Cause? Risk?	1. Vision Objective? Vision Reward?	1. Vision Link?	- Current Alternatives and Plans?
2. Problem? Cause? Risk?	2. Vision Objective? Vision Reward?	2. Vision Link?	- History? - Action Constraints?

This chart will drive your Value Mining efforts. It will guide the questions you ask as well as give you a sequence to ask them. In the next few chapters we will take the problems you solve and the visions you enable and build a detailed MVP questioning strategy, but first let's look more closely at how to make a questioning strategy successful.

Earning the Right to Ask

As you are well aware, prospects will not be willing to share their problems unless they can see a payoff. That's why you want to come to a prospect meeting prepared to add value immediately by thoroughly knowing the prospect's company, industry and market trends. Obviously, the more you know about the prospective client and the more you can anticipate problems and threats to the prospect, the better prepared you will be to Value Mine and the more credibility you will gain to bridge the value gap.

Jim Greene is a Vice President at Cap Gemini Ernst & Young (CGEY) and heads their Global Financial Services Sector. His clients are the CEOs of the largest financial institutions in the world, who pay CGE&Y and firms like it hundreds of millions to billions of dollars for outsourcing and consulting services. At this level, you can't wait for the meeting to determine motivation. As Jim says,

"I will only pursue ten deals this year. By the time I meet with the CEO, I have to know a good deal about his industry, his business and his problems. I read everything from their financials to their brochures. Clients are not willing to wait for or pay for your diagnostics. The days when you could spend six months figuring out the problem and then two years implementing your solution are a thing of the past. They want creative and prescriptive answers with payoffs starting in six months. "

In addition to being ready to respond intelligently to whatever a prospect shares about his or her performance objectives, changes and threats, you will want to be able to share insights into the potential client's company, industry and competition.

As one service buyer from a Fortune 100 company put it, "I will always meet with someone who can tell me something I did not know about my company or industry."

Successful service providers frequently use these insights as the pretext for a meeting, saying something like, "John, we have just completed a cost study of the electronic components industry. I think you'll find some of the results interesting. When would be good time to get together?"

Give-and-Take Questions

Armed with quality research on the prospect, effective business developers use what I call **Give-and-Take Questions** to initiate an information exchange with potential clients. A give-and-take question is a two-step question that first offers information or insight about the prospect's company, industry or competition (Give) and then asks the client to share information (Take).

By using the give-and-take questioning technique, you establish your credibility by sharing your knowledge and insights in exchange for your prospect's comments about his or her objectives and obstacles.

Here are a couple of examples of give-and-take questions:

- *The article in* The Wall Street Journal *said you were looking to Asia for 20 percent of your growth next year. Have your objectives changed given the recent currency destabilization?*
- *Our research indicates that well over half of the mergers in this industry fail. What do you see as the obstacles in your merger strategy?*

Some service providers use a more formal give-and-take approach. For example, investment bankers will frequently arrive armed with a financing strategy "pitch" to create credibility and interest. The key is to keep it interactive. As one banker told me, "If I am going to pitch a variable rate financing, I want to know about the client's previous experience with them before I bring it out. If I find out that they were burned, I'll keep my recommendation in my pocket."

The give-and-take technique is particularly useful for potential clients who are initially reluctant to share their problems and want you to show your hand first. Prospect reluctance (or your preoccupation with your pitch) may force you into a premature and vendor-centric presentation of your capabilities or ideas. Try not to fall into this trap. Whenever possible, turn the presentation back into an exchange.

In the next two chapters we will use the MVP questioning strategy and the give-and-take tactics to find and build motivation and vision and then to uncover and reduce resistance to your solution.

Chapter 5:
Glossary of Terms and Key Concepts

Premature Solution Syndrome - The tendency of service providers to see a prospect's problem and offer a solution before the prospect is ready to take action and before the service provider fully understands the prospect's situation. This reduces your value in the eyes of the client, because at this point the perception of pain is greater than the prospect's yet to be developed motivation and vision.

The Importance Of Questions - If you are going to be their partner, a prospect wants you to understand their unique circumstances and be personally invested in their objectives. You need to know the prospect's motivation, vision and location in the decision-making process. The prospect needs to know if you are capable, different and trustworthy before he or she will provide the information you need. Questions create a rational and emotional exchange that demonstrates your capabilities and also: 1) encourage prospects to share critical information, 2) build their perception of need, 3) reveal their likelihood for change, and 4) locate the prospect in the decision process.

MVP Question Strategy - Converts your MVP Value Proposition into questions that allow you to determine and practice what to ask when in your Value Mining efforts.

Give-and-Take Questions - A two-step question that first offers information or insight about the prospect's company, industry or competition (Give) and then asks the client to share information (Take).

Chapter 6

Find and Build Motivation:
A Reason to Leave Current Practices

Client Transformation Decision

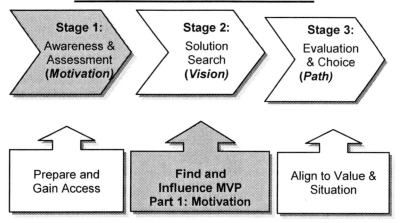

Your Value Mining Strategy

Without motivation, no transformation decision will occur and therefore no service provider will be chosen. In this chapter, we go deeper into uncovering motivation. You will begin to use your MVP Questioning Strategy to encourage prospects to share problems, which will, in turn, enable you to find and build motivation. This will also put you in a position to better predict whether a potential client will move forward with a transformation decision. Through this process, you can quickly qualify prospects and allocate your resources wisely.

You will recall from our anatomy of a transformation decision that motivation is the fuel that creates the initial momentum for change. Without the motivation to fix something, solutions hold no value. The first thing you want to uncover with your questioning strategy is whether a potential client perceives a threat (or opportunity) that your services can address. To find and build motivation, use your questioning strategy to complete the four steps described below:

1) Find obstacles to performance and personal objectives that you can support.
2) Explore causes.
3) Identify and expose the long-term consequences of the obstacles.
4) Assess motivation to determine if the prospect is qualified.

You will notice that the question pattern parallels the first column of the Service Value Chart you developed in Chapter 4. We will use it again to find and build vision in the next chapter. First, let's take a closer look at the steps in finding and building motivation.

1) Find Obstacles to Performance Objectives

When problems threaten objectives, motivation for change builds and a search for solutions begins. To help build your motivation questioning strategy, think about what threats to success you have helped current clients mitigate. In other words, what problems have you solved for current or past clients?

Next, think about what questions you would ask to elicit information on those problems. For example:

- What has changed in your prospect's marketplace?
- What are your prospect's performance objectives for this year?
- What is this company trying to do, and why can't it do it?
- What is preventing the individual you're meeting with from gaining power, prestige, pay or professional satisfaction?
- Which of these problems can you help with and how?

Remember, obstacles to personal and performance objectives are the seeds of change. The executive search firm discussed in Chapter 4 determined that their prospect would be worried about a delay in the execution of their business plan without key employees in place. A possible motivation question the search firm might have asked the prospect would have been, "How have unfilled key positions affected the timing of your execution?".

Here is a sample give-and-take question relating to performance objectives:

I noticed that you have been able to cut your product development cycle by 43 percent. That gave the stock a nice boost last year. Is there still more efficiency to be gained there, or will you focus more on top-line growth this year?

Here are examples of give-and-take questions to uncover obstacles to objectives:

The four-wall contribution of your newer stores is about 10 percent less. How will you maintain your margins as you expand into second-tier markets?

Many of my clients are worried that the pace of change is accelerating, but their ability to respond is limited. How will you stay agile in volatile markets?

2) Explore Causes

What are the causes of the problems that have threatened your clients? What questions would you ask to see if a potential client shared that view? Once again, if you took a stab at creating an MVP Value Chart, look to vision links for cause-related questions. Using the search firm example again, a cause question could have been, "Why is it taking so long to get the executive team in place?"

3) Identify and Expose Risk of Status Quo

To build motivation further, expose for the prospect the long-term consequences of not addressing these threats. In other words, what is the **status quo risk** or the risk of not doing anything at all? What status quo risk questions might you ask that would lead a prospect to consider those consequences?

The search firm might ask what impact a delay in hiring or a bad hire would have on results this year. Other examples of questions that explore status quo risk are:

How will declining four wall contributions affect your long-term performance?

What happens if you can't meet your integration timetable?

4) Assess Motivation: Is This Prospect Qualified?

What's worse than a potential client who says "no?" The answer is prospects who won't say "yes" *or* "no." Have you ever had a client who seemed very interested in your service but never made the final decision? You made presentations, wrote and rewrote proposals, even attended meetings and social events – all to no avail.

As any good poker player will tell you, it's not the worst hands that are expensive. You fold the bad hands quickly and only lose your ante. It's the hands that are good, but not quite good enough, where you lose your shirt.

Once you've established that the prospect does have a problem you can fix, you need to probe for information on how important that problem is (**criticality**) and when the prospect thinks it has to be fixed (**urgency**). Criticality and urgency are obviously related, but urgency can be the service provider's best ally.

Even situations that are not normally critical can become so if there is a deadline. Have you ever put everything on hold to get a last-minute present for your spouse? Or perhaps you have left an important meeting to make one of your children's events. The folks who flood the stores on December 24 know all about how urgency can drive criticality.

As urgency increases, the prospect's inclination to act increases and the inclination to shop alternatives and fight for the last dollar in the deal decreases dramatically. *Always establish a time frame* with the potential client. If there is no urgency, there is no engagement.

Is this prospect motivated to make a transformation decision? Is it time to explore solutions or should you wait until the situation is more urgent? To help you make that call, you can use the **Change Motivation Scale** I introduced in Chapter 2. The scale gauges a prospective client's potential for change and helps service providers determine how to respond appropriately. Some of my clients also use this scale to help them categorize prospects for forecasting purposes.

Change Motivation Scale (and Response)

Obstacle Intensity	Urgency Indications	Change Potential	Response
Unknown	No interest	Dormant	Withdraw, Passive contact
Nuisance	Awareness, Low priority, Low urgency	Latent	Withdraw, Passive contact
Problem	Assessment but no schedule	Possible	Explore status quo risk, Establish urgency, Active contact
Threat	Action commitment; deadline set	Probable	Determine resistance, Explore solution alternatives, Deadline? Momentum recommendations, Continuous contact
Crisis	Taking action; Urgent deadline	Certain	Determine resistance, MVP Presentation

Dormant or Latent Motivation

Potential clients who currently show no recognition or interest in discussing or overcoming an obstacle have no motivation to act on your recommendation. Perhaps they don't perceive a threat, have other priorities or have already addressed the problem to their satisfaction. If, in response to your queries, the prospect shows neither interest in nor recognition of the obstacle, their change potential is dormant.

In this situation, your best course of action would be to withdraw and maintain passive contact. The occasional call, e-mail or article of interest mailed to the prospect will keep you on their radar screen in case their level of motivation changes. The same response is warranted for prospects who recognize obstacles but consider them low priorities.

Service professionals frequently fall back on the "shotgun approach" when faced with prospects with low potential for change. They return to a vendor-centric presentation, racing through their capabilities in front of disinterested listeners, hoping one of those capabilities will strike a chord. This approach is neither effective nor dignified.

In cases where the prospect is not interested or is actually negative, withdraw gracefully and turn your attention to a new prospect. Remember, the prospect is not rejecting you; this issue is simply not a priority for this prospect at this time. It may become a priority in the future.

In such cases, you might say to the potential client, "I can see you have a number of issues ahead of this one. It's possible that this may become a priority in the future. Do you mind if I stay in touch with you about it?" If you approach dormant or latent prospects this way, they will likely be relieved that you're sensitive to their other priorities and you will build the foundation for a future relationship.

If you do maintain passive contact, you may be considered an incumbent when and if they decide to take action since the prospect will already be familiar with you. In addition, you will have already developed some degree of credibility through a flow of helpful but unobtrusive communication.

Possible Motivation

Issues that have been identified as problems (as opposed to "nuisances" or "threats") by the prospect can go either way. These issues have the potential client's attention, but change is just a possibility. No timetable exists. The prospect has one foot on the accelerator and one on the brake. Change is possible, but so is the potential for wasting your time.

Most potential clients have a long list of unresolved issues. Solutions take time and are expensive to implement for such complex issues. Therefore, if the obstacle is a problem, you can attempt to increase its status to a threat by exposing the long-term status quo risk. Find out what will happen, and to whom, if this problem is not fixed.

Items classified as problems on the Change Motivation Scale have a low probability of action unless the resistance to a solution is also very low, i.e., unless you can fix the problem reliably, quickly and inexpensively. You may be able to un-bundle your services and offer them in smaller increments that fit the prospect's current motivation level.

Alternatively, you can offer services that would migrate the potential client stage by stage through the transformation deci-sion. For example, you could offer diagnostic services to a firm that is assessing obstacle risk. Perhaps you could offer a market analysis to a company that is exploring alternatives. We'll take a closer look at how to do this in Chapter 8 in a discussion on **Momentum Recommendations**.

Probable Motivation

Threats are easier to read and deal with. Someone within the organization has already uttered the equivalent of Apollo 13's "Houston, we have a problem."

In these cases, urgency and criticality are high; thus, change is probable. The company is either committed to or is in the process of transforming. You will want to uncover resistance issues, explore solution visions, outline a path toward resolu-tion, make momentum recommendations and maintain continuous contact with a prospect in this motivational stage.

Certain Motivation

Crisis requires immediate action, so you, as the service pro-vider, should take the bull by the horns. Uncover resistance issues and make a presentation using the MVP format described in Chapter 9. Initiate the engagement, offer immediate action and work out the terms as you go. Be careful because crisis driven solutions frequently fail because they are often implemented without clearly defined objectives and consensus. That can lead to dissatisfaction.

Finding and Building Motivation—In Action

Here's a composite real-life example that shows how Value Mining for motivation works. A successful partner of a consulting firm that provides location-forecasting models invited me to join him on a meeting with the vice president of real estate for a large apparel company. The partner started with a brief presentation overview but smoothly turned the discussion to changes in the market and the VP's performance objectives and obstacles.

When asked about his performance objectives, the real estate VP talked about the challenge of continuing to grow (performance objective) while maintaining margins (performance objective). The partner revealed that other clients found that a few non-performing stores cannibalized the margins of the rest of the company (give-and-take question) and asked about the VP's experience. The VP told us that a few non-performing stores could have a significant impact on the bottom line (obstacle).

The relationship manager then asked the VP to describe the difference between an average-performing store and a poorly-performing store. The VP told us that an average-performing store brought in $1 million a year more than the weak performers. When asked about the long-term consequences (status quo risk), the VP revealed that a location mistake couldn't be resolved quickly because any new store was usually locked into a seven to ten year lease. That meant that each "mistake" location cost $7 to $10 million, and that 10 percent of existing stores fell into the under-performing category. Finally, the prospect agreed that screening out weak locations before stores were built (problem converted to vision objective) was a priority.

By questioning instead of presenting capabilities, the partner was able to find and build on the prospect's motivation for change. He asked about obstacles to performance objectives and then found that the status quo risk of not addressing the problem represented millions in lost profits.

The location consulting firm partner did a good job of finding and building motivation. It seemed clear that bad locations posed a significant threat for this prospect. The VP of real estate was aware that bad locations created a drag on earnings. The consulting partner even got the VP of real estate to agree to a proposal presentation in front of the CFO and CEO. Was that the appropriate next step or a premature solution? We will find out in the next few chapters as we continue to look at how to Value Mine to build vision and reduce path resistance.

Chapter 6:
Glossary of Terms and Key Concepts

Status Quo Risk – The risk continuing on the same path, i.e., if no transformation decision is made. Status quo risk questions build motivation for change by exposing the long-term consequences of not addressing a problem.

Criticality – A prospective client's perceived importance of a particular problem. Urgency and criticality are related as one influences the other.

Urgency – The timeframe by which the prospect believes a particular problem must be fixed. As urgency increases, the prospect's inclination to act increases and the inclination to shop alternatives and fight for the last dollar in the deal decreases. Successful service providers always establish a time frame.

Change Motivation Scale – Provides a guide for gauging a prospective client's potential for change and helps service providers determine how to respond appropriately.

Dormant or Latent Motivation – The prospect lacks recognition of or interest in discussing or overcoming an problem. The prospect is unaware, doesn't care or has already addressed the problem. A service provider's best course of action is to withdraw and maintain passive contact.

Possible Motivation – An obstacle to an objective that the client views as a problem, but perhaps not a priority. Change is possible and no timetable exists. A service provider can attempt to increase its status to a threat by exposing the long-term status quo risks or offer a scaled down version of the service.

Probable Motivation – The obstacle is perceived as a threat. Urgency and criticality are high, and change is probable.

The service provider will want to explore solution visions, uncover resistance issues and outline a path toward resolution, make momentum recommendations and maintain continuous contact with a prospect in this motivational stage.

Certain Motivation – A crisis requiring immediate action results in the prospect's complete commitment to resolving the problem now. The service provider should quickly uncover any resistance issues and begin the engagement immediately.

Chapter 7

Build Vision and Reduce Path Resistance:
A Better Place to Go and a Safe Way to Get There

Client Transformation Decision

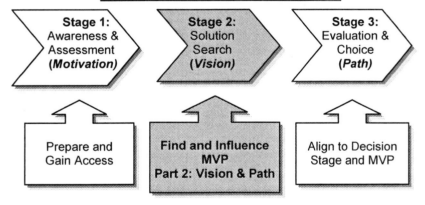

Stage 1: Awareness & Assessment *(Motivation)*	Stage 2: Solution Search *(Vision)*	Stage 3: Evaluation & Choice *(Path)*
Prepare and Gain Access	**Find and Influence MVP Part 2: Vision & Path**	Align to Decision Stage and MVP

Your Value Mining Strategy

Once motivation has been established, it is time to move to the next phase of your MVP Questioning Strategy to build clarity and consensus for your vision and to uncover and reduce resistance to your proposed path to resolution. To build vision, use your MVP Questioning Strategy to:

1) Convert problems to **Vision Objectives** to make them actionable.

2) Ask **Vision Reward** questions to strengthen the attraction for change.

3) Ask **Vision Link** questions to build preference for your solution.

To uncover and reduce path resistance –

1) Review the prospect's current alternatives and plans.

2) Explore the prospect's history: examine previous attempts to overcome the obstacle and the results of those efforts.

3) **"Yellow pad" solutions** to preview the prospect's response to your recommendation.

4) Determine **action constraints**.

Recall that once a problem has become a critical and urgent threat to the prospective client, a search for solutions begins. The prospect knows he or she can no longer continue on the same path and remain successful. A new destination must be found before any transformation decisions can be made.

As the vision of a better future gains clarity and consensus, that vision itself motivates transformation. At this point in the transformation decision process, the potential client migrates from a problem to a solution focus. New performance objectives are established, and a search starts for ways to overcome the causes and avoid the status quo risk.

To support this migration your MVP Questioning Strategy should:

1) Convert problems to **Vision Objectives** to make them actionable.
2) Ask **Vision Reward** questions to strengthen motivation for change.
3) Ask **Vision Link** questions to build preference for your solution.

Let's look at the types of questions you would ask at each of these steps.

Problems to Vision Objectives

The first step in migrating from problem to solution search is to establish a solution target. Where are we going? A prospect who tells you that margins are tight is not ready for change. A prospect who says he is looking to improve margins is moving toward a solution. A prospect who has established new margin-enhancing objectives and a deadline for achieving them is well along in the solution search process.

What questions would you ask a prospective client to convert problems to vision objectives? The executive search consultant may ask, "What is your timeframe for filling this position?" The location consultant could ask the real estate VP, "Is reducing location mistakes a priority for this year?"

Vision Reward Questions

The more the prospect sees the reward for solving a problem, the more it creates purpose in the prospect's mind. Such perceived purpose offsets the pain of a solution. Instead of presenting the benefits of a solution, help the prospect build his or her perception of value by asking Vision Reward questions such as, "What will fixing this problem mean to you?"

The search firm would ask what it would mean to the client to have its executive team in place sooner. The location consultant, would ask what it would mean to reduce bad location selections.

Vision Link Questions

Converting problems to objectives gets the prospect moving toward a solution, and Vision Reward questions build the attraction of solving the problem. Vision Link questions encourage prospects to move toward *your* solution. Your motivation questions explored causes to problems. Vision Link questions build preference for your path for addressing those causes. Let me give you a couple of examples.

Recall that the search firm's client was worried that they could not execute their business plan without the executive team in place. Once that objective had been established, the search firm could begin building preference for its solutions with Vision Link questions like, "Would it help you to have faster access to a larger pool of candidates?" This question links the prospect's Vision Objective with the search firm's database of candidates. As you can see, the service provider is conducting an MVP Presentation using a questioning strategy that builds value in the mind of the prospect before a proposal is made.

Here is another example. The real estate VP said an objective was to increase margins. The location consulting partner asked if it would be helpful to be able to identify weak locations in advance. This Vision Link question prepares the prospect for the consultant's ability to predict location performance.

Find and Reduce Resistance to Your Path

Recall that transformation value is equal to purpose minus pain. So far you have done all you can to increase value by finding and building purpose (M&V). To build maximum transformation value and preference for your solution path, the next step is to uncover and then reduce the prospect's perception of the pain associated with your solution.

Before you pull the trigger on your recommendation, find out if there is anything that would cause the prospect to resist your proposal. There are many reasons why potential clients may be unwilling or unable to commit to your solutions. These include:

- **Motivation Awareness and Consensus** - In a multi-decision maker environment, if each stakeholder does not share motivation, criticality and urgency, your recommendation will encounter resistance.
- **Vision Clarity, Awareness and Consensus** - Some prospect stakeholders may not be aware that a solution is available, may not have or share a clear alternative vision or may not understand how your solution differs from current or previously proposed (or tried) remedies.
- **Competition** - If the problem is a threat or crisis, chances are that the prospective client is already evaluating internal and external alternatives to your solution.
- **Bias** - Previous attempts, either failures or successes, may bias the prospect toward an alternative method or against your proposed solution.
- **Cost** - Cost includes not only the price of your service but also the time and internal resources necessary to implement your solution.
- **Solution Risk** - The prospect may be unsure about whether you will be able to do what you say you can do and may worry about what happens if you are wrong.
- **Inability** - The potential client may be unable to decide or act because of insufficient authority, budget limitations or internal process requirements. I call these action constraints.

Each of these potential roadblocks can add friction to the decision process and potentially lower your value in the mind of the prospect. By uncovering these issues before you make your recommendation, you can adjust your message or service to reduce friction. There are four steps for uncovering and reducing solution risk:

1) Review current alternatives and plans.
2) Explore the prospect's history: examine previous attempts to overcome the obstacle and the results of those efforts.
3) "Yellow Pad" solutions to preview the prospect's response to your recommendation.
4) Determine action constraints.

Taking these four steps should expose any perception of risk in your solution and allow you to make adjustments to your recommendations so that you will be in step with the prospect and remain aware of any resistance that exists. Here's a closer look at each step.

Review Current Alternatives and Plans

If things have reached the threat or crisis stage, the prospect has probably already taken some action or is preparing to take action. It would be helpful to know what vision alternatives are being considered or what progress has been made. Ask questions such as:

- Have they already decided on a solution?
- Have they decided to get help?
- Have they made a service provider decision?
- What is being done now and how is it working?

Explore the Prospect's History

Chances are that your prospective client has addressed the same or similar problems in the past. It's important to learn about these previous efforts for several reasons. First, it will enable you to learn more about the prospect's decision-making process. Secondly, if the previous efforts did not go well, you may uncover the cause of the prospect's resistance to trying again. You will want to determine:

- What previous attempts were made to resolve this problem?
- How and why was the decision made?
- Who was involved in making the decision?
- What was the outcome of the decision?
- What would the client do differently this time around?

"Yellow Padding" the Solution

The danger of offering a solution before a potential client is motivated to make a change is not only that it's more likely to fail, but also that it may inoculate your prospect against further recommendations. Once someone has said "no," any persistence that you exhibit will seem pushy and may make the prospect inclined to defend his or her negative decision.

An excellent way of avoiding this problems is to preview your proposal informally using a tactic commonly referred to as **"yellow padding"** before making a formal recommendation. With this technique, you say something like, "Before I give you my proposal, I'd like to review with you what I'm thinking." Then, outline your recommendation for your prospect on a yellow pad (or on a white board).

Since solutions informally outlined on a yellow pad are viewed as hypothetical solutions, prospects can react to them without fear because they don't require taking a stand. In other words, they provide you with a non-threatening way to preview the reaction that your formal proposal will receive. Uncovering resistance points and problems now helps you deal with them before making your formal presentation and keeps you in sync with your prospect's position in the decision-making process.

A further benefit of this method is that by the time you reach the written proposal stage, you will already have gained agreement on its essential contents. Thus, in effect, your proposal has been thoroughly discussed in the yellow pad format beforehand; all the prospect needs to do upon receiving your actual proposal is to sign on.

Determine Action Constraints

A friend of mine works for a company that compiles and sells commercial real estate sales data to companies that use it to value property. The company was approached by a state government agency that wanted to use the company's services for property assessments, and they subsequently signed a contract with the agency – one of the largest contracts of the year.

Unfortunately, as my friend discovered, the expenditure had to be put into a budget that would not be approved until the following summer. Even though the sale ultimately went through, the loss in forecasted income disrupted the firm's revenue forecasts for the year and negatively affected its stock price.

Often, as this example shows, it's not a prospect's willingness to make a transformation but his or her inability to do so that knocks a potential engagement off track. These **action constraints** – the things that prevent a company from acting on a transformation decision – may include lack of authority, budget limitations or processes requirements.

Nothing is worse than spending months with a receptive prospect only to find out that he or she doesn't have the authority or budget to make a decision. Ultimately, the questions you must answer to determine which, if any, action constraints are present in any given situation, are:

- Can this person make this happen? If not...
- Who would need to be involved in the decision? (Value mine with every stakeholder in the decision.)
- Where would the money come from?
- How would the decision proceed?
- What is the urgency?

Each step of the Value Mining process brings you and your potential client closer to both a transformation decision and a service provider decision. In preparation for your proposal, you will align your recommendation to the both the prospect's decision stage and to their MVP as we will do in the next two chapters.

Chapter 7:
Glossary of Terms and Key Concepts

Vision Objectives Questions – Converts problems into actionable solution targets that are measurable and move the prospect from problem-oriented thinking toward solution-oriented action.

Vision Reward Questions – Elicit from the client the benefits of transforming to a new vision that further strengthens the motivation for change and begins to outweigh pain of change.

Vision Link Questions – Build preference for your solution and unique capabilities. They establish a link between the prospect's need and *your* proposed solution.

"Yellow Padding" Solutions – An informal preview of your recommendation that uncovers potential resistance before a formal presentation. They provide you with a non-threatening way to preview the reaction that your formal proposal will receive. Uncovering resistance points and problems early helps you deal with them before making your formal presentation and keeps you in sync with your prospect's position in the decision-making process.

Action Constraints – Limitations that prevent a company or individual from acting on a transformation decision. Some action constraints may include lack of authority, budget limitations or company process requirements.

Chapter 8

Momentum Recommendations:
Aligning to the Decision Stage

Client Transformation Decision

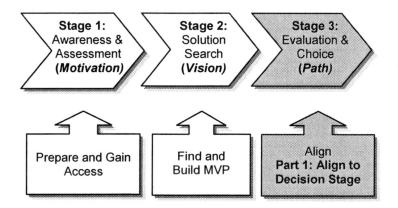

Your Value Mining Strategy

Selling professional services is a multi-call, multi-decision maker process. If proposals are not aligned with the prospect's decision stage, they will cause friction and slow or stop the process. In order to avoid premature solutions and to keep the process moving, successful service providers offer **Momentum Recommendations** that:

1) Align with the prospect's current stage in the transformation decision process,

2) Advance the decision

3) Require the prospect to act now.

Once you have found and influenced your prospect's motivation and vision and uncovered potential resistance to your path, it is time to prepare a proposal aligned to the prospect's MVP. Before you do so, make sure your proposals are also aligned the prospect's **Transformation Decision Stage**. Failure to do so may undermine your efforts to this point.

As you will recall, the relationship manager in our earlier example was invited to make a proposal to the real estate VP, the CFO and the CEO of the prospect company. In preparation for his proposal presentation, the location consulting partner used his notes from his meeting with the real estate VP to create a unique MVP Value Chart for this client. This became the foundation of his proposal presentation. The chart looked like this:

MVP Service Value Chart

Problem	Vision/ Objective	Vision Link	Service Capability	Proof
Non-performing stores hurting margins. Losing $1 million per year for 7-10 years.	Improve Margins	Screen out week locations in advance Predict sales by location	Client profiling and forecasting models	Reduces location mistakes by 75%

When the day came to make his proposal, the partner felt confident that this prospect would soon be a client. After he was introduced to the CFO and CEO, the manager launched into his proposal presentation.

"Steve, you said that your margins are being negatively impacted by under-performing stores whose four wall contribution is $1 million less per year than your average store (motivation). Further, your lease provisions prevent you from mitigating the problem for seven to ten years, leaving you with a $7 to $10 million loss per store (status quo risk).

"We can help you improve your margins going forward (vision) by significantly reducing the location mistakes before stores are leased and opened (vision link). That's because you will be able to more accurately predict sales by location using our profile and forecasting models. Clients who have used these models have reduced location mistakes by 75 percent (proof)."

At this point in the presentation, the CEO turned to the real estate VP and said that as far as he was concerned, the problem with the under-performing stores was not so much the location as it was the weak managers in those stores. To that, the CFO revealed that a consultant she had retained suggested the problem was with the merchandising. The three executives continued to make their conflicting cases on the *causes* of poor store performance using up most of the presentation time.

What happened? The relationship manager had done a good job of uncovering the real estate VP's motivation and had aligned and presented his proposal presentation to it. But was it time to present a solution? Not quite.

Although the VP of real estate was ready, it is clear that he was not the only decision-maker. He was part of a decision-making team that included both the CEO and the CFO. These three executives had not even reached a consensus on the cause of their problem; furthermore, they did not share a common vision or agree on a path toward resolution of the problem. In a multi-decision-maker environment, you need to Value Mine with *all* of the stakeholders and attempt to create a **Consensus MVP**.

It was now clear that the consulting partner had offered a premature solution. So far, he had uncovered the motivation and vision of only one of the stakeholders. He had learned nothing about other sources of potential resistance to his proposed solution.

Is there consensus on motivation and vision? Is it urgent? What were they doing about it now? What had they tried before? How did it work? Who made the decision? How? The partner had not gotten the answers to any of these critical questions before presenting his proposal.

Aligning to the Decision Stage:
Momentum Recommendations

As this case illustrates, value mining professional services in the invisible market is a complex interaction. Not only do you have multi-level decision-making, but the multi-call process can take months.

A **premature solution** occurs when a proposal is presented during the wrong stage of the transformation decision. In the example above, the partner made a proposal before there was consensus on motivation. That happened because he failed to identify all of the decision-makers and Value Mine with each of them.

To overcome this multi-level, multi-call challenge, successful sellers use what I call **momentum recommendations** to align themselves with the current stage of the prospect's decision-making process, to build commitment and to keep the process moving toward a successful conclusion.

"Let Me Write Something Up for You"

Has this ever happened to you? You successfully helped your prospective client see the risk of continuing to do things in the same way. The prospect seemed interested in your vision solution, so you tell the prospect you will put something in writing and get back to her. You send in your proposal and wait for a response. Nothing. You call. No response. You wait an appropriate period. You reach her voice mail. "Ellen, I just wanted to follow up on that proposal...." No response.

When this happens to you, it's because the excitement of finding motivation distracted you from completing your value mining with the prospect and converting value into action through a momentum recommendation. As soon as you left the prospect's office, your biggest and most dangerous competitor – the status quo – won back your prospect's attention and affection.

A potential client's motivation to act peaks during face-to-face meetings. Your presence shines a light on a problem and a possible resolution. If you do not convert that motivation into action, you may have lost your best opportunity to win the business. At the very least, by failing to keep momentum and gain commitment, you have extended the decision and potentially opened the door for your competitors.

Transformation decisions are typically complex and can take months or even years to culminate in the choice of a service provider. By keeping the engagement process moving forward, you increase the likelihood of success and reduce your cost of sales. As we have seen above, presenting a proposal prematurely causes friction.

A proposal is the last step in Value Mining, but that does not mean you cannot build agreement and commitment along the way with momentum recommendations. A proposal should be a restatement of the MVP that you and your potential client create in collaboration. It is in that respect your final momentum recommendation.

Building momentum and commitment over an extended decision process requires making recommendations in person that:

1) Are in alignment with the prospect's current stage in the transformation decision process,
2) Advance the decision
3) Require the prospect to act now.

Momentum recommendations continually advance the engagement, build motivation, clarify and build preference for your vision and path, and build commitment by having the potential client take immediate action. Progress should be measured by where the prospect is in the transformation decision process and what the client must do to move forward.

It's up to you to determine what a realistic recommendation is for the prospect at any given point in the process. In other words, given the company's current motivation, vision clarity and consensus, preference and resistance, what can you realistically recommend that will build commitment and momentum?

Locating Your Prospect on the Transformation Decision Map

As we outlined in Chapter 2, transformation decisions tend to follow a pattern. If you can recognize that pattern and locate your prospect in the process, it will be easier to make appropriate recommendations that advance the engagement. Again, here are the stages to a prospect's transformation decision:

Transformation Decision Stages

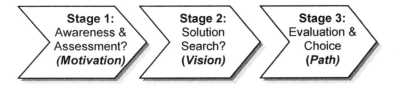

To help our location consulting partner get back on track, let's determine what transformation decision stage his prospective client is in. To answer that question, let's locate the VP of real estate on the transformation decision map.

Awareness? Yes
Assessment? Yes
Solution Search? Unknown
Solution Evaluation? Unknown

It is clear from this prospect's decision map that the partner has offered a solution that is premature even for the VP of real estate. Had he invested more time in building a preference for his vision and uncovering potential resistance to his path, the partner may have discovered that other decision-makers would be involved. He might also have become aware that another consultant had already been retained and had, in fact, proposed an alternative solution. The partner may also have uncovered a different cause to the problem.

The consulting partner and the prospect had not yet explored a shared vision of a better future. Instead of offering to make a proposal presentation, the partner would have been better served by recommending further discussion with other stakeholders about the causes and potential solutions. This prospect needed a momentum recommendation to fit this stage of the transformation decision.

This example demonstrates that once you've determined where prospective clients are in the transformation decision process, you can set objectives for your follow-up with them, including momentum recommendations to help prospects move to the next phase of the process. For example, if the prospect is aware of the obstacle but has not assessed the status quo risk, what would you recommend they do?

If such a prospect is clearly motivated and a consensus exists, but the prospect remains uncertain or unaware of alternatives, how would you recommend they build their understanding and preference for your vision solution? How could you help them build clarity and consensus in your plan to resolve the threat? What would you recommend to help them move from agreement to commitment to execution?

Fortunately, the location consultant from our case study recognized that his proposal had not taken the CEO's and CFO's motivations into consideration and quickly adjusted his approach. Instead of proposing that this prospect use his services to support new location decisions, the location consultant offered a momentum recommendation that actually shortened both the transformation and the service provider decision. He built consensus for using his service capabilities to help resolve the key motivation question: What was causing the poor performance of certain under performing stores?

The consultant recommended that the client work with his firm to conduct a limited study that would compare location factors from both the best and worst performing stores. According to the consultant, such a study would isolate the role of location in store performance. The prospect agreed to the smaller project and, in the interest of time, did not shop the recommendation. The location consultant had successfully helped the client build consensus and had gained a commitment to use his services.

Setting Meeting Recommendation Objectives

Whenever you meet with a prospect, establish for yourself in advance what the potential minimum and maximum momentum recommendations might be and practice them. Make sure you have a recommendation in mind even if it is only to set another meeting. What is the outcome (vision) of the recommendation and why would that be of value to your prospect?

Try using the "so what?" technique to extract the value to the client. How will you explain the steps (path) of your recommendation to build clarity and comfort that the outcome will be achieved? Again, urgency is your strongest ally. Look for impending events and gain agreement on a deadline or at least a timeline. Plan your meeting to assure you have time to present, discuss and make a plan for implementing that recommendation.

Now it's time to make your final momentum recommendation, the proposal presentation. In the next chapter, we will use your **Service Value Chart** to create a powerful proposal.

Chapter 8:
Glossary of Terms and Key Concepts

Transformation Decision Stage – One of three phases in a prospect's transformation decision process. The stages include:

- *Stage 1: Motivation Stage* - Awareness and Assessment. The company becomes aware of or begins to perceive a threat (or opportunity). Assessment of the threat is initiated; if the threat is considered significant enough, a search for alternatives begins.
- *Stage 2: Vision Stage* - Solution search. The company envisions and searches for possible solutions to obstacles uncovered in Stage 1.
- *Stage 3: Path Stage* - Solution evaluation and choice. Alternative solution paths are evaluated, and the company commits to one and takes action.

Momentum Recommendations – Recommendation offered by the service provider which are closely aligned with the prospect's current stage in the transformation decision process, are intended to advance the decision and require the prospect to act now. Proposals not aligned with the prospect's decision-making process will cause friction and slow or stop the process.

Consensus MVP – The coming together or alignment of various stakeholders to create a common motivation, vision and path to resolution.

Premature Solution – Occurs when a solution is offered or a proposal presented at the wrong stage of the prospect's transformation decision. This may occur when a service provider fails to value mine with all stakeholders in the decision.

Chapter 9

Aligning Your Proposal:
Preparing the MVP Proposal Presentation

Client Transformation Decision

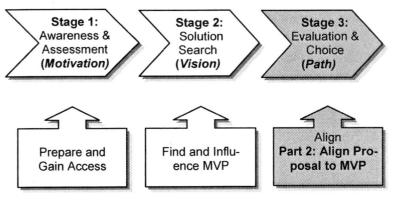

Your Value Mining Strategy

Your prospect is now ready for your final momentum recommendation – your proposal. Continue building a solid partnership by showing that you are aligned to the prospect's MVP. To do this, turn your MVP Value Chart into a simple, yet powerful **MVP Presentation**, as described in this chapter.

The prospect has now reached the final stage of the transformation decision-making process. It's been a long road, so let's review how we got here. The graphic below summarizes how we used Value Mining to reach this point.

Value Mining Questions and Action Strategy

Motivation	Vision	Vision Link	Service Re-sistance
Question Strategy			
1. Problem? Cause? Risk?	1. Vision Objective? Vision Reward?	1. Vision Link?	- Current Alternatives and plans?
2. Problem? Cause? Risk?	2. Vision Objective? Vision Reward?	2. Vision Link?	- History? - Action Constraints?
Action Strategy			
- Assess Motivation	- Assess Vision Clarity & Consensus	- Align to Decision Stage	-"Yellow Pad" Proposal
-Momentum Recommendation	-Momentum Recommendation	- Value Align Proposal	-Present MVP Proposal

Now that you have completed your Value Mining and know that the prospect's decision makers agree on motivation, vision and path (MVP), you have now earned the right to present your proposal and ask for commitment. Most importantly, the prospect should be prepared to see the value of your service and recommendations. In short, the value gaps have been closed.

It is now time to align your proposal with this prospect's MVP by converting it into a highly effective MVP Proposal Presentation. To see how this is done, let's convert the executive search firm's MVP Value Chart we highlighted earlier in the book to an MVP Proposal Presentation. Their Value Chart looked like this:

MVP Proposal Presentation

Motivation   Vision   Path to Resolution

Motivation or Status Quo Risk	Vision Objective	Vision Link "That is because"	Service Capability	Proof
Weak executives create drag on growth	Hire best people	- More choice of candidates - Larger candidate pool	Extensive database	References, highest client satisfaction in survey
Unfilled key position hurting our performance	Execute strategy sooner	- Fill position sooner - Faster access to candidates	Extensive database	35,000 executives in database
Don't want to waste time with candidates who don't fit our culture	Hire best fit	- Only interview good fits - Screens out misfits	Candidate screening tools	25 percent faster placement on average
Don't have the time or access to do it myself	Better use of my time	-We can handle it for you -Proven process	25 years in business	75 percent reduction in placement turnover

As you'll recall, the MVP Value Chart was assembled by asking "So what?" until we connected the search firm's service capabilities to the potential client's problems and vision for the future. To develop an MVP proposal presentation from the MVP Value Chart, we work in reverse order – from the client's motivation to a shared vision to the search firm's path to resolution. Once again, instead of working from your service to the client's need, we start with what is important to the client and show how your solution fits that need. That makes the presentation client-centric and more relevant. So, instead of asking "So what?" we use phrases like "That is because..." to create vision links from the prospect's objectives to the search firm's services.

Instead of saying, "Mr. Client, we can offer you an extensive database, proven screening tools and the unparalleled experience of 25 years in business," the executive search firm would present its proposal in a client-centric MVP presentation as follows:

"Mr. Prospect, you mentioned that weak executives created a drain on your company's growth *[Motivation]*. We can help you hire the best people *[Vision]* because you will have more choices from a larger pool of candidates *[Path to Resolution]*. *That's because* we maintain a large database of executives to support our searches. The database includes profiles and resumes of 35,000 screened executives.

"You also mentioned that unfilled key positions were making it difficult for you to begin executing your strategy *[Motivation]*. We can help you execute your strategy sooner *[Vision]* by filling this key position *faster [Path to Resolution]*. *That's because* the database gives you instant access to a large pool of qualified candidates. Our searches are completed 25 percent faster than the industry average."

This search firm takes the potential client's problems of *weak people, wasted time* and a *drag on performance and growth* (motivation) and offers a vision of *executing a business strategy sooner* by *hiring the best people faster* without wasting the client's precious time. The search firm also provides a clear path to resolution with the vision links of *faster access, better choices* and *a reliable process* because of their service capabilities. In addition, it provides *experience, a database, screening tools* and proof in the form of *size* and *proven performance*.

Create Your MVP Presentation

You can turn your own Service Value Chart into an MVP Proposal Presentation. Once you are done Value Mining with a prospective client, restate your prospect's problem, cause and risk (Motivation), convert it to a vision objective (Vision), then provide a clear Path to Resolution by vision linking with phrases beginning with *"That is because"* and offer proof to reduce resistance. It will probably sound awkward at first, but, as you practice, you will gain comfort and confidence.

Creating this MVP Proposal Presentation is the final step in transforming your original vendor-centric sales message into a format that is completely client-centric and that aligns with this prospect's MVP and situation. If you have done a thorough job of aligning to the prospect's position in the transformation decision-making process, then the result of your MVP Proposal Presentation should be a positive one.

Even with a solid Value Mining strategy, competition is frequently unavoidable. In the next chapter, we look at what happens when a prospect wants to evaluate competitive alternatives in the visible market. Specifically, we'll discuss how you can use strategic empathy to respond to this opportunity and win new business.

Chapter 9
Glossary of Terms and Key Concepts

Value Mining Questions and Action Strategy

Motivation	Vision	Vision Link	Service Re-sistance
Question Strategy			
1. Problem? Cause? Risk?	1. Vision Objective? Vision Reward?	1. Vision Link?	- Current Alternatives and plans?
2. Problem? Cause? Risk?	2. Vision Objective? Vision Reward?	2. Vision Link?	- History? - Action Constraints?
Action Strategy			
- Assess Motivation	- Assess Vision Clarity & Consensus	- Align to Decision Stage	-"Yellow Pad" Proposal
-Momentum Recommendation	-Momentum Recommendation	- Value Align Proposal	-Present MVP Proposal

MVP Presentation – A means of leading the prospect toward your particular solution by adapting information gathered through Value Mining and recorded on the Service Value Chart. An MVP Presentation restates the prospect's problem, including its cause and risks associated with action (Motivation), converts it to a vision objective (Vision) and provides a clear course of action (Path to Resolution) by vision linking with phrases beginning with "*That is because,*" and finally offering proof that reduces a prospect's resistance.

Part II:
Winning in the Visible Market:
Supporting the Service
Provider Decision

Most service providers feel that they can't abandon the visible market entirely. Competition may be unavoidable even for projects that you have escorted through the transformation decision. In Part II you will see you how successful service providers win competitive service provider decisions in the visible market by finding and then aligning to the prospects rational and emotional alternative comparison process.

Chapter 10

Chart Your Preference Value:
Communicating How You Are Different

I n competitive situations in the visible market, if a prospect cannot see or does not value the characteristics that make you different, a preference value gap threatens your ability to win the business. Just as you used an MVP Value Chart to establish a client-centric message in the invisible market, you can use a similar tool – a **Preference Value Chart** – to identify and articulate the differentiating characteristics that make you the provider of choice among a field of competitors. This chapter shows you how to chart your preference value.

When a prospective client moves into the visible market to compare competitive alternatives, your value is no longer based solely on whether you can help them make the transformation. Now, your value proposition must also include the things that make you different and better than the prospect's alternatives. In the visible market, you have to: 1) show the service buyer that you can help fulfill their MVP, and 2) convince them that you can do that better than anyone else.

If you've done a good job value mining with a prospect in the invisible market, you will have gone a long way toward fulfilling the first part of that assignment. You established preferred provider status when you supported the transformation decision. That creates a significant competitive advantage over other firms that are only now getting acquainted with the pro-spective client.

Once the prospect moves into the visible market and has other choices, the possibility of a preference value gap increases significantly. As you'll recall from Chapter 1, a preference value gap occurs in the visible market when your prospect makes the decision to use a service you provide but prefers a competitor to you.

Preference Value Defined

Before describing how to close the preference value gap, let's define the term. Simply stated, preference value is the difference between the winner's value and the loser's value to the prospect. Thus, winning in competitive situations is all about establishing preference for your services over that of your competitor by align-ing the things that make you different and better with the prospect's rational and emotional selection criteria.

Preference value, like service value, is in the eye of the be-holder. All that matters is what the buyer thinks is valuable. If you offer more services than your competition, but the buyer does not value these expanded options, you will have increased your costs and squeezed your margins but gained no competi-tive preference.

Preference Value Gets 100 Percent of the Business

A small difference in preference value can be the key to winning or losing; there are no awards for finishing second. As the prospect's alternatives increase, preference value increases in importance.

For example, an executive I interviewed admitted that she chose one service provider for a $300 million contract over a competing firm that offered a better-known name but similar vision, path and price because the winning service provider "seemed a bit more responsive." Even though the price of the service was $300 million, the better-known competitor lost 100 percent of the business for lack of a few phone calls. Differentiation is the key to winning when there is choice.

Consider this simple personal example. I spent $40,000 on my last car. I chose my car over the alternative brand because I thought it was faster and I preferred its styling to others in its class. I ended up paying about $2,000 more than the next closest brand. Had the price difference been much more, I may have chosen brand X. My preference value then was five percent ($2,000/$40,000). That means that 100 percent of my purchase decision was made on a five percent difference in value.

I chose to buy the car from the nearest (most convenient) dealer who was $150 more expensive than a lower priced but less convenient dealer. So 100 percent of the dealer choice was based upon a 0.4 percent preference value.

Of course, services are much more difficult to compare than products, so there is a little more room to establish preference. Keep in mind, however, that as soon as the prospect has a choice, preference value becomes 100 percent of the decision. As the number of potential vendors increases for the prospect, the differences that separate you from competitors typically narrow.

Even though in the eyes of the prospective client you are 99.9 percent as valuable as the preferred provider, you lose 100 percent of the business if you aren't able to establish your preference value. This is why creating preference value, even if it's by the slimmest of margins, is so crucial to your ultimate success.

We lost on price?

"They gave us the best price."

You didn't listen. Your presentation was confusing. I am not sure you were committed. You went around me. Your references didn't support you.

In any service provider decision, the majority of competitors lose. The reason most service providers cite? "We lost it on price." Claiming to have lost on price saves face for a rejected service provider. For companies buying a service, telling the losing bidders that price was the deciding factor is also the easy way out. They don't risk offending anyone by saying that they didn't think a service provider could do the job, and they avoid getting into arguments with vendors about the real reasons they chose the winning firm.

If price were the real reason for losing, that would mean that the winner won on price. But how often have you heard someone say they won because of price? When price is the deciding factor, it is because the service buyer worked through the buying hierarchy: right solution, right people, trust and right fit and perceived no difference between the finalists. If you say you lost on price, you are really saying you were unable to differentiate your service to justify your higher price or your price premium. In fact, in most cases, the reason for losing out to competitors is not price; instead, it is the failure to establish preference value in the mind of the service buyer. We will revisit buying hierarchy and price again in the next chapter.

Why Do Clients Prefer You?

Just as you did with the MVP Value Chart, use the Preference Value Chart below to isolate your service characteristic, define what is unique about that characteristic, align the characteristic to the potential client's motivation and decision criteria and add evidence to increase confidence.

Preference Value Chart

Unique Service (Branded)	Differentiator (Equalizer)	Preference Value Link ("So What?")	Proof

As you can see, this chart has four columns:

- The **Unique (Branded) Services** column isolates and names your service or the theme of your service.
- The **Differentiators** column explains the uniqueness of your solution or service capabilities.
- The **Preference Value Link** column links your unique solutions or capabilities to the prospective client's decision criteria by asking "So what?" until you have reached a selection criteria or vision objective.
- The **Proof** column presents evidence that adds credibility and confidence to your preference value message.

Here are some of the questions you'll want to answer as you complete the **Preference Value Chart**:

- What image or brand would you like to create in the minds of prospective clients?
- How would you like your current clients to describe you to others?
- What is it about your people, process, service capabilities, or reputation that distinguishes you and is difficult for your competition to match?
- Most importantly, why is your solution and path more reliable and convenient than alternatives?

Anyone who has ever bought a service or sought to deliver a service knows that visions are easy, but execution is hard. Therefore, if you can distinguish your service on the reliability of its execution, this will give you the most leverage and the best chance of eliminating a preference value gap.

Building Your Preference Value Chart

To build your Preference Value Chart, begin with the *Unique Services* column. What do you offer that is unique, difficult for competitors to duplicate, important to the prospect and increases the likelihood that the service buyer's objectives will be achieved? Isolate and, whenever possible, name (brand) that capability characteristic. Naming it or giving it a brand further distinguishes this characteristic from alternatives and makes it easier for potential clients to remember.

Under *Differentiators*, list what makes your solution or capability different or unique. Next, complete the *Preference Value Link* column by asking "So what?" to align your differentiator with the prospective client's motivation and resistance. Keep asking "so what?" until you reach one of the prospect's comparison criteria or objectives.

If you haven't met with the prospective client while they were in the invisible market, use the objectives and criteria set forth in their RFP or other materials provided.

Finally, complete the chart by adding under *Proof* any evidence to build confidence in your differentiator. This might include statistics, references that speak directly to your service differentiator or a detailed competitive comparison.

Here's an example of Preference Value Charting in action. I worked with a commercial real estate company whose only offices were in New York City. This company was having difficulty winning competitive business against large national concerns. When I asked them how they described their services to potential clients, they talked about how they were committed to good service, had good market knowledge, offered full service expertise, had two NYC offices and had seasoned professionals in their employ. Initially, their Preference Value Chart looked like this:

Preference Value Chart

Unique Service (Branded)	Differentiator (Equalizer)	Preference Value ("So what?")	Proof
Committed to good service Good market knowledge Full service expertise NYC offices			

These are all excellent attributes but hardly unique. What company doesn't say they work hard, offer good service and have experience? The best this firm could expect to do with such an undifferentiated message would have been to finish tied with another nondescript company. All things being equal, most service buyers will choose the market leader over such an ill-defined company.

All the same, this firm's existing clients loved them, so I

asked what they had done for their existing clients that set them apart from the national companies. They indicated that it was the experience of their service professionals that differentiated them from their competitors.

How is that different? (Differentiator)

"Most of the nationals pitch the business with the experienced brokers, but the work is actually done by junior people who work on transactions all over the Northeast. In our case, all aspects of the transaction are handled by professionals with at least 20 years of experience in New York City. Our clients never have to deal with rookies."

So what? (Preference Value Link)

"Most New York properties are sold or leased to other New Yorkers. We know the market, and we know how to execute the deal. We know who is active, what they are looking for and what they can pay. We have all done hundreds of deals, so we can get it done with fewer mistakes and fewer surprises."

So what? (Preference Value Link)

"Once the client decides to sell or lease a property, they want it completed as soon as possible. Slow execution exposes them to market risks and ties up their funds. Our clients receive faster and smoother execution from us, which translates into less market risk and more liquidity."

Can you give evidence that your experience gets these better results? *(Proof)*

The real estate firm was able to demonstrate consistent disposition execution in 90 to 120 days. The firm also provided proof in the form of references from existing clients that compared their performance to national firms. Furthermore, the firm branded their execution capabilities "No Rookies Execution" to emphasize their unique transaction experience. Now take a look at their Preference Value Chart:

Preference Value Chart

Unique Service (Branded)	Differentiator (Equalizer)	Preference Value ("So what?")	Proof
"No Rookies Execution" Team	Deal only touched by someone with at least 20 years of NYC experience	Faster execution, Fewer mistakes More liquidity	Comparative references 120 day dispositions Resumes

Now, instead of listing good service, knowledge, expertise and local offices, this real estate company presented an image of a more reliable execution along these lines:

"Our *'No Rookies Execution'* means that you and potential investors will only deal with a professional who has had at least 20 years of experience in New York City. That means higher quality representation, faster execution, fewer mistakes and more liquidity. That also means no more hand holding junior staff through the process. On average, our dispositions close within 120 days of initial marketing. Here are the résumés of our *No Rookies team.*"

The real estate firm focused on the reliability of their execution. Instead of going firm on firm they matched up individual players. They were able to turn weakness into strength. Prospective clients might have assumed that the larger firm would give them a more reliable execution, but the *"No Rookies"* brand made the nationals seem less reliable. National firms may be broader, but a local firm could be deeper and more experienced in a specific market – this was the message the real estate firm successfully communicated. It was now the national firm whose execution seemed less reliable.

In preparing your preference value message, you want to find and align all of your service differentiators and have them ready in your sales and marketing arsenal. You also want to be prepared to explain how other characteristics of your service are as good as competitive alternatives. I call these comparisons **equalizers**. Each prospective client will have different selection criteria, and you want to be prepared to align your presentation accordingly.

However, when presenting your preference value, try to focus on a single theme. Trying to position yourself as the best in everything dilutes your brand and your credibility. If possible, choose a theme that focuses on reliability and convenience of execution tailored to the specific prospect.

The Total Value Chart

To create your total value proposition, combine your Preference Value Chart with your MVP Value Chart. Now, in addition to answering, "What can you do for me?" you can answer two additional questions from prospects, "How are you different?" and "Why is that important to me?" Here is what a **Total Value Chart** looks like:

Total Value Chart

Service Value   Preference Value
(What can you do for me?)   *(How are you different?)*

Motivation	Vision	Vision Links	Service? (Branded)	Differentiator	Preference Value	Proof

The more you know about how and why prospects make service provider decisions, the easier it will be for you to align yourself with a prospect's MVP and win new business. In the next chapter, we'll look at why and how service buyers actually make choices among firms competing for their business.

Chapter 10:
Glossary of Terms and Key Concepts

Preference Value – The prospect's perceived difference between the winner's value and the loser's value. Preference value is that small distinction that makes you better than an alternative in the mind of the client. It is strengthened by aligning those things that distinguish you from the competition with the prospect's rational and emotional selection criteria.

Preference Value Chart – A tool used to identify and articulate the rational differentiating characteristics that align your capabilities with the prospect's comparison criteria. The preference value chart takes your services, identifies what makes it different and valuable to the client and then offers proof.

Total Value Chart – A tool that combines your service and preference value charts to provide a total value message. It helps the service provider answer the prospect's key decision questions:
"What can you do for me?"
"How are you different?"
"Why is that important to me?"

Total Value Chart

Service Value   Preference Value
(What can you do for me?)   *(How are you different?)*

Motivation	Vision	Vision Links	Service? (Branded)	Differentiator	Preference Value	Proof

Chapter 11

The Visible Market Decision:
Understanding the Service Provider Decision

Prospects use formal comparisons of service providers to make better decisions, to gain better terms or to adhere to internal policy requirements. In this chapter we explore the three phases of the **Service Provider Selection Process**: the **Search Phase**, the **Screening Phase** and the **Selection Phase**. We will show how the prospect advances through each phase.

The service provider decision occurs in the last stage of the transformation decision. The prospective client has become aware that there is a problem, has assessed the problem's criticality and urgency and has searched for solution alternatives. Now, in Stage 3, the prospect is evaluating and choosing among alternative paths offered by service providers. A formal selection process is indicated by the request for proposal (RFP), request for quote (RFQ) or statement of qualifications (SOQ).

Informally, these processes are referred to as beauty contests, shoot-outs and bake-offs.

Why a Formal Service Provider Comparison?

There are three primary reasons for using a formal comparison process to choose a service provider. Companies may use a formal service provider comparison to make better decisions, to secure better terms or because a company's internal policy requires a more transparent process to reduce risk. The assumption many prospective clients make is that having more options leads to better decisions. Let's look more closely at the reasons companies use a formal comparison process.

Better Decisions

When faced with an infrequent or first-time purchase, companies often feel they need more information to make a good decision. Companies buying a service for the first time don't know how to choose, what to choose or who to choose. They also do not have the time or resources to become an expert on the service provided by you and your competitors. Because of limited resources and limited knowledge, these companies let competitive forces identify what is important, what is different and what is preferable. Their decision criteria remain fluid and evolve throughout the decision-making process.

Better Terms

The primary reason for competitive comparisons is to attain the best terms. This is particularly true with familiar service provider decisions. When companies have been through the process before, have a clear vision and path and believe competitors offer similar capabilities, they will be more inclined to seek better terms.

These repeat buyers will resist your efforts to engage them in the invisible market. Because they tend to view service provider capabilities as being similar, they are usually looking for pricing and service-level leverage. Broader choice creates more supply than demand. Market forces assure the best services and prices.

Reduce Decision Risk

Service provider selections made at the executive level expose decision-makers to a great deal of risk. If the chosen provider does not perform well, it could reflect negatively on the decision-maker. Decision-makers are in some cases turning over the keys to their careers to the service providers they choose; therefore, emotion and risk reduction play prominent roles in the final choice.

That explains why execution reliability is so important to prospects and also provides insight into why companies frequently make the safe choice even when it is not the best choice. This need to reduce risk gives market leaders a big advantage. If a company chooses the market leader and something goes wrong, it's the market leader's fault. But if a company executive takes the risk of not choosing the market leader and something goes wrong, it's perceived to be his or her fault for not making the safe choice. Formal provider selections reduce the risk of making a poor decision by spreading responsibility across an organization and by imposing a transparent discipline to the process.

The Formal Decision Funnel

The formal service provider selection process can be described as a funnel where criteria are used first to increase choice and then to eliminate alternatives until the final selection is made. The decision process typically progresses this way:

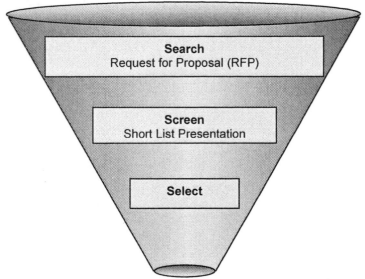

The three phases of the service provider selection process are the **Search Phase**, the **Screening Phase** and the **Selection Phase**. Inclusion or exclusion in each phase is based upon decision criteria that become increasingly selective and subjective. The number of provider candidates eventually narrows to a single winning service provider. Let's take a closer look at what happens in each phase.

Search Phase: "All of The Usual Suspects"

Decision criteria during the Search Phase are inclusive and designed to gather as many alternatives as necessary to assure (and demonstrate) a good decision. Inclusion is based upon the purchaser's awareness of and access to service providers with relevant capabilities. Service providers will recognize the Search Phase as the RFP (request for proposal) or SOQ (Statement of Qualifications) stage of the process. The objective is to maximize choice by including anyone who is potentially qualified to help.

Screening Phase: *Selecting Out Alternatives*

The Search Phase frequently uncovers too many choices to be individually evaluated. The objective of the Screening Phase is to winnow the group down to a manageable "short list" for closer evaluation. At this point the decision becomes a rational comparison process. Standards for comparing similar characteristics are set, and these criteria are used to eliminate some potential vendors and establish preference among the remaining alternatives. Standards are tightened to eliminate all but the three or four "short list" competitors who most closely align to decision criteria.

As mentioned previously, criteria for new or infrequent decisions are constantly changing as the service buyer learns more about their problem(s) and its (their) potential solution(s). For routine decisions, criteria tend to be more stable and rigid. Survivors of the Screening Phase often include the least risky (market leaders and incumbents) for reliability, least expensive for price leverage and the most innovative for idea leverage. Frequent service purchasers will often skip the first two phases and invite only the "short list" firms to speed the process yet win the best terms.

Selection Phase: *First Among Equals*

The first two phases of the selection process are rational and, if done well, offer the prospect an opportunity to make a decision on a more subjective basis. The "short list" candidates are invited to meet the decision-makers and present their cases. Anyone who has made it this far is well qualified, so decision criteria expand beyond capabilities to the unique rational and emotional fit of one provider over the rest.

The criteria used to narrow the short list to the chosen service provider are usually subjective and based on emotional reactions that may include confidence, comfort and trust. The service provider's demonstrated understanding of the unique aspects of the client and the engagement builds confidence. Comfort speaks to the personal compatibility of the provider and client. Do they like each other? Trust is elicited from the demonstrated commitment to see the engagement through to a successful completion. These subjective attributes are impres-

sions and are largely communicated non-verbally. If the purchaser perceives no differences between suppliers, low price
will be used to determine the winner.

Buying Hierarchy

If the client company perceives that it has at least
one comparable rational and emotional alternative,
price will become the determining criteria. Remember
that price differential, like value, is in the eyes of the
beholder. Some clients view a 10 percent price varia-
tion as comparable; others view even one percent as a
premium. Although most service providers believe that
price is the dominant decision factor, research indicates that price only becomes important if the client
has choice among several providers who offer equal
value in more important criteria areas like reliability.

Don Potter is the CEO of Strategy Street, a management consulting firm. He has been studying customer
buying habits since he started with McKinsey in 1973. According to Potter, the importance of price is overestimated.
"When customers buy," he says, "they consider first product function, then reliability and convenience, and finally
price.

"*On average*, across all markets, price is the deciding
factor in less than 15 percent of all sales. The customer
buying process reflects a hierarchy of needs, each of which
must be met to the customer's minimum required level before he moves on to consider the needs at the next level."

In the service environment, I would translate that needs
hierarchy as:

• **Vision:** Is it the right solution vision? If it works, will
the vision fix the problem? The solution must first address
the company's motivation for making the transformation
decision. It doesn't matter how reliable, convenient or
inexpensive the solution is if it doesn't solve the problem.

• **Execution Reliability:** Can and will this service provider deliver? The service buyer must believe the provider can and will deliver on promises they deem important.

• **Convenience:** How easy or how difficult will it be, how long will it take, how disruptive will it be and what inconveniences will be involved? If a provider's solution is too difficult or too disruptive to implement, it would add to cost and risk.

• **Price:** What does it cost? What is the best price offered to meet all identified needs related to this problem?

Price leaders only win when the price difference is substantial in the eyes of the buyer and when the low-price candidate can meet minimum standards for execution reliability. Saving a little money on a price leader whose performance is uncertain is too risky.

The price leader's role for the client is to provide pricing leverage. Once the service buyer has won price concessions from the preferred provider, the price leader's role in the service provider selection process is over. The process can become expensive in terms of time and resources for price leaders as they are often kept hanging on until final negotiations have been completed only to lose in the end.

Chapter 11:
Glossary of Terms and Key Concepts

Service Provider Decision – The final stage (Stage 3:Path Stage) of the decision-making process during which a prospective client is evaluating and choosing among alternative paths offered by service providers. In earlier stages the prospect has become aware that there is a problem, has assessed the problem's criticality and urgency and has searched for solution alternatives.

The Formal Decision Funnel – A description of the formal service provider selection process, where criteria are used first to increase choice and then to eliminate alternatives until the final selection is made.

Search Phase – A phase during which the prospective client gathers as many alternatives as necessary to assure a good decision outcome. Inclusion is based upon awareness of and access to service providers with relevant capabilities.

Screening Phase – A phase during which the prospective client narrows the list of competitors through a rational comparison of vendors. Standards are progressively tightened to eliminate excess choice.

Selection Phase – The final phase during which the prospective client meets with a "short list" of providers that have demonstrated expertise and capabilities. Final decisions are typically made using more subjective criteria such as comfort, confidence and trust.

Chapter 12

Preference Value Mining:
Establishing Rational and Emotional Preference

This chapter shows you how to successfully survive each phase of the **service provider decision** to become first among equals. You build awareness to get invited, find and align to the prospective client's decision criteria to build **rational preference** and preview your working relationship and collaborate in order to build **emotional preference**.

Service Provider Decision Stages

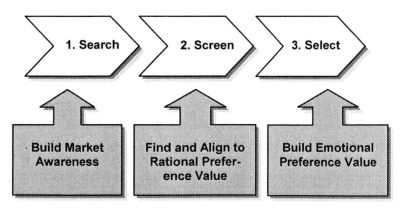

Service Provider Competitive Strategy

Search Phase: *Get Invited!*

You can be the most capable service provider and have the most innovative ideas, a proven process and competitive pricing, but you cannot win competitive business unless you get invited to participate in the search process. And you can't get invited unless the service buyer knows you exist. This means you need to be recognized and easy to find, which requires elevating your personal and corporate **market profile**.

Maximum demand for your services will occur when all of the people who need your service know that you provide it and know how and where to contact you. The higher your market profile, the more likely you'll be invited to participate in the search phase.

Advertising, publicity and direct mail keep your firm name and brand in front of potential clients so that you do get invited to participate in formal selection processes. However, unless you are part of a small firm, you may not have influence over corporate branding, positioning, advertising and marketing. But you can establish a personal brand that is enhanced with references, speeches, articles, publications and direct contact with potential clients.

The good news is that your personal brand becomes more important as the prospective client moves deeper into the selection process and becomes more concerned about such things as confidence, comfort and commitment. So if you can get invited into the process and avoid being screened out too early, you may have the opportunity to tilt the playing field in your favor before the selection is made.

Pick Your Battles

Responding to an RFP typically drains a firm of 40 to 100 man-hours, but on larger projects it can balloon to hundreds of hours. Multiply those hours by salary and overhead and suddenly you have a very expensive investment. One outsourcing executive told me his firm will spend $2 million in pursuing a single opportunity. More and more companies are holding professionals accountable for their cost of sales when calculating utilization and revenue production. This is particularly true of public companies.

Instead of responding to every RFP that comes along, ask yourself whether your time would be better spent building a preferred or sole provider position in the invisible market.

Many service professionals feel they have no choice but to respond to RFPs. They say, "We have to respond, or it would send the wrong message to the market." Or "You have to kiss the frog a few times before it turns into a prince."

The idea is that you have to work your way up the hierarchy on a vendor list. Despite the low "hit rate," kissing lots of frogs seems justified to these providers. Most of the time, service providers respond to RFP's because they are not aware of the invisible market or do not know how to participate in it. If you are going to compete in the visible market, at least choose your battles wisely.

The point is to look at the RFP response as an investment. Ask yourself what is the expected value of the response. What is the likelihood of winning multiplied by the revenue, or, better yet, profit value of the engagement? Would that time be better spent establishing an incumbency with a prospective client versus taking a long shot on a beauty contest?

To pick better battles, ask yourself these questions about each RFP:
- Do we have an existing positive relationship with the client?
- Do we have unique skills, capabilities, or resources that are critical to the project's success and difficult for competitors to copy?
- Does the client recognize our unique value proposition?
- Do we have access to the client before submission or presentation of our proposal?

If you answered "no" to two or more of these questions, you may want to choose a better prospect, one who is better aligned with your value.

Use the time saved to build an incumbency with a new client or migrate an existing client to a new project. The sales cycle is longer because clients will be earlier in their decision process, but the "win rate" is much higher.

Screening Phase: *Preference Value Mining*

Your capabilities and experience made you initially attractive during the Search Phase, but this may not be enough to sustain you through the Screening Phase when the service buyer's goal is to create a short list of service providers that most closely fit its transformation MVP.

Your task during the Screening Phase is to determine the buyer's decision criteria and to position your capabilities to align to those criteria. This is what I call Preference Value Mining. The three steps for preference value mining are:

1) Find this prospect's preference value (i.e. decision criteria),
2) Build preference for decision criteria that fit your differentiators
3) Align your proposal to this client's MVP and preference value.

1) Find This Prospect's Preference Value

Although your capabilities got you invited, they must now be aligned to this prospect's decision criteria to maximize your chances of surviving the Screening Phase. Find the decision criteria either through direct discussions or by inference based on provided information. Ask these questions:

- What are the decision criteria?
- How are the criteria prioritized?
- How will they be measured or evaluated?
- Who will make the final decision? When?
- Who is the competition?
- Is there an existing relationship?
- How does the prospect view your competition's strengths and weaknesses?

Most of the questions that you need to answer deal with your firm's previous results and experience, innovative ideas and price. During this stage, prospects are asking themselves: Can they do it? Can they do it for us? Will they do it for us? Will it work? Will it be hard? Is it risky? Execution reliability is a critical component to prospective clients.

The best way to avoid being "voted off the island" during the Screening Phase is to uncover the selection criteria and to align your vision and capabilities to the prospect's stated or implied selection criteria. Many service buyers, particularly those who are in the market frequently, will not allow face-to-face meetings until the field is narrowed to a more manageable "short list." This makes it difficult for you to find the prospect's MVP, criteria and situation.

Without personal interaction, the prospect's elimination criteria will be limited to the rational, "Who meets our criteria?" side of the decision. If you are forced to determine criteria by inference, look for the motivation behind the questions asked in the RFP. Focus on execution reliability. The first priority of most service buyers is to identify the service provider that can help them reach their vision objective reliably. What makes you the safest choice?

2) Build Preference for Criteria That Fit Your Differentiators

Sometimes the prospective client is not aware of or does not understand and appreciate what is different about the services you provide. If you are able to meet with the potential client during this stage, use your Preference Value Chart to build a questioning strategy that will build awareness and preference for your differentiators. If the client resists a face-to-face meeting at this stage, your preference value chart will still help you demonstrate how you are different, but you will have to wait until the selection phase to execute your preference value mining strategy.

3) Align Your Proposal to This Client's MVP and Preference Value

Whether through direct discussions or through inference, the more you can align your proposal with your prospect's MVP and preference value, the more likely you will survive the rational screening process. Use your Total Value Chart developed in Chapter 10 to create a proposal that most closely aligns you to this prospect's decision criteria.

Understanding the service buyer's decision criteria allows you to align your service and presentation. It also gives you more latitude to influence decision criteria and to offer alternative visions and paths. Consider the following example.

A San Francisco Bay area water utility district was looking for a design consultant for a seismic retrofit for its pipes and storage facilities. The decision criteria were routine and focused on the bidder's experience designing ground-shaking reinforcement.

A southern California design firm that worked primarily with oil and gas clients had recently opened a San Francisco office and wanted to compete for this business. With limited experience with the water utility district and with the type of project involved, the firm's prospects didn't look bright until they explored the transformation decision that preceded it.

In their face-to-face meeting with the water utility district's staff the consulting firm discovered that the integrity of the pipes and storage facilities was essential to fire-fighting capabilities after a major earthquake. Given the essential nature of the project, the southern California firm then asked questions about the effectiveness of only addressing ground-shaking risks.

Specifically, this service provider asked if the client had considered the impact of fluid forces within the tanks – something they knew a great deal about since they had designed energy storage tanks. The utility district had not considered fluid dynamics and agreed that it would be critical.

The newcomer from southern California won the business because they did more than just answer the RFP questions. They explored the transformation decision, found the decision criteria and then built preference for their differentiators. That helped both to strengthen the client's MVP and to improve the vendor's chances for winning the contract.

Just as we did in Chapter 6, look for motivation and resistance when exploring the transformation decision. Ask:

Motivation?
- What changed in the prospect's situation?
- What is the status quo risk that motivated the decision to transform?
- What will be the consequences if no change is made?
- What is the criticality and urgency?

Vision?
- What is their vision of a solution?
- How will the vision bring the company to resolution?
- Does the vision have clarity and consensus?

Path?

- What is their potential resistance to your solution?
- What are they currently doing?
- What did they do and how did they do it in the past?
- What was the outcome?
- Are they aware of and do they understand your vision and path?
- What are the decision constraints?
- What are the decision criteria?

Selection Phase:
Comfort, Confidence and Commitment (Trust)

If you reach the Selection Phase, it is because you have successfully differentiated your capabilities from those service providers that were screened out. All of the service providers on the short list are well qualified, so your professional qualifications probably won't differentiate you during this final stage.

The winner in the Selection Phase will be chosen based upon emotional preference value: subjective and non-verbal decision criteria that include comfort (charisma and familiarity), confidence (the service provider's understanding of the client's needs and situation) and commitment (the service provider's demonstrated commitment to the client and the project). In a word, trust.

Instead of focusing on what is different about you (vendor-centric), build emotional preference by focusing on what is different about the prospective client (client-centric). If you have not supported the transformation decision or had previous contact with this prospect, it is critical to establish **emotional preference** by demonstrating your emotional alignment and commitment to the client's transformation MVP. Once again, use your service value and preference value mining skills to understand the prospect better than your competitors do. This builds confidence in you and your services.

To build trust, engage the client personally. Instead of telling the potential client what you are going to do, give a preview of what a working relationship with you *feels* like. Actually start the engagement. It takes the same time and effort as saying what you are going to do but gives you and the client a head start.

In summary, awareness and capabilities get you invited, rational differentiation keeps you in the game, but it is emotional differentiation that gets you selected. Throughout the Search Phase you can use your vendor-centric pitch to build credibility and get invited. To survive the Screening Phase you will need to become client-centric in order to determine and rationally align your proposal to the service buyer's decision criteria.

To win the Selection Phase make as much personal contact as possible to determine MVP and demonstrate your understanding of the potential client and commitment to the project. In other words, collaborate to build emotional preference value. Show them that you would make a good partner.

Your one-on-one contact with the prospect during the Selection Phase should improve your hit rate in competitive situations, but as we will see in the next chapter – even if you win the business, you can still lose the engagement.

Chapter 12:
Glossary of Terms and Key Concepts

Market profile – Your recognition and reputation in the market. The higher your market profile, the more likely you'll be invited to participate in a competitive comparison. Market profile is enhanced through advertising and publicity at the firm level and speeches, articles and meetings at the individual level.

Preference Value Mining – Process of finding, influencing and aligning to the prospect's rational and emotional comparison criteria. Preference Value Mining entails: 1) finding a prospect's criteria, 2) building preference for decision criteria that fit your differentiators, and then 3) aligning your proposal to this client's MVP and preference value.

Emotional Preference – Subjective and non-verbal decision criteria that include comfort (charisma and familiarity), confidence (understanding of the client's needs and situation) and commitment (the service provider's demonstrated commitment to the client and the project). In a word, trust.

Chapter 13

Team-centric Relationships:
Winning the Engagement

Becoming client-centric through strategic empathy leads to more business, but winning the business is different from winning the engagement. **Winning the engagement** means successfully completing the project and, by doing so, creating the best possible source of future business—a delighted client. To win the engagement, you will want to establish a **team-centric relationship** with all of the client stakeholders.

One of the primary differences between selling a service and selling a product is that the service professional sells something that does not exist until after the sale. The prospective client cannot see it, smell it, taste it, drive it, wear it or measure it before the engagement contract is signed. Service professionals offer their expertise to client executives in a collaborative process that leads to outcomes or a shared vision of a better future.

No professional business service can be successfully completed without the active support and participation of the client. In the service world, the buyer is a co-manufacturer of the work product, and the role of the buyer is integral to the achievement of the vision and to the success of the service provider. In addition to selling, the service provider must also deliver, execute and maintain the service relationship. So, in effect, the sales process does not end until the assignment is completed.

Results that don't meet expectations create dissatisfaction, increase costs and undermine the potential for follow-on business and referrals. The client's staff and employees usually have to bear the pain of the path. If the client's staff does not buy into the project, they can find a thousand ways to undermine it and blame it on you. For example, the head of a large healthcare concern tells of a $400 million computer installation that failed because the users would not use the new system.

Once the contract is signed, you will want to establish a **team-centric relationship** with your client. To assure project success, everyone should be pushing towards the same goals in a cooperative and collaborative way. This is accomplished by expanding your Value Mining activities to include stakeholders in the client project.

If you followed the Value Mining process, you built clarity and consensus in the vision at the decision-maker level. To win the engagement, you will need to broaden consensus and clarity to include all client stakeholders, particularly the execution team. The staff may believe that this project is good for management and good for you, the service provider, but they may very well be asking what's in it for them.

How do you address change resistance in staff? Go through the same value-building process that you did with the decision-makers. Change management is similar to selling; people must see a good reason to give up current practices (motivation), have a clear understanding and consensus for the vision of a better future (vision) and see a path that provides a safe and reliable way to get from here to there (path to resolution).

Build a common cause partnership with all stakeholders by individually finding, influencing and aligning your methods to their motivation to change and their vision of a better future. Lack of understanding, predictability or collaboration will lead to resistance or, worse, sabotage. In contrast, a shared purpose goes a long way to make the pain of attaining the vision acceptable.

Once you have gained buy-in to the common cause, assure active participation in the path by developing a clear execution plan with consensus and commitment to objectives, deliverables, timeframes, roles and responsibilities. Now everyone will know why they are going, where they are going and what they need to do to get there. By creating a common cause you not only gain more resources to reach the vision, but the client is more tolerant of delays and problems because you are facing them together.

Building a Client Sales Force

The best way to avoid selling is to have your clients do it for you. Successful engagements result in delighted clients, and delighted clients willingly become your surrogate sales force. Happy clients give you more follow-on business and refer you to new prospects. This means you spend less time selling, but you win more business than ever before.

Chapter 13:
Glossary of Terms and Key Concepts

Winning the Engagement – Successfully completing a client project, thereby creating the best possible source of future business—a delighted client.

Team-centric Relationship – A collaborative relationship with all stakeholders in the prospect organization. Winning the engagement is facilitated by value mining with client stakeholders to build a common cause and shared responsibilities.

Final Thoughts

Unlike your counterparts in the capital goods arena, service providers are not groomed at an early age to sell. Whereas capital goods salespeople move out of sales to join the executive ranks, service professionals become senior executives by taking on more revenue responsibility as their careers mature.

At its core, providing a service means helping. You became a service professional because you wanted to use your expertise to help clients achieve their objectives. Although you are well paid, client appreciation is the intrinsic compensation that brings the most career satisfaction. When you are forced to deal with people who don't know or appreciate you, it causes anxiety, uncertainty and even anger.

Business development is a necessary evil that allows you to do what you enjoy most, helping. In these difficult times, you spend most of your time worrying about selling instead of helping clients. You are asking questions like these:

- How am I going to make my numbers this year?
- How will the market find out about our services?
- How do I get access to decision-makers?
- How do I convince prospective clients that ours is the best service?
- Why aren't they moving on our proposal?
- Why aren't they returning my phone calls?

The objective of this book is to help you sell less, win more and exercise more control over this critical part of your career. My premise is that the more you are aligned with prospective clients, the more likely you are to win their business. This is more important than ever in these turbulent times.

The more you know about how and why the service buyer makes the decision to use a certain service or the decision to choose a particular service provider, the more you can align your message and service solution to fit the client's need, situation and decision-making process.

I am convinced that mastering the art of value mining makes it faster and easier to penetrate, qualify and capture the invisible market. It will also improve your hit rate in the visible market. To survive and prosper in a tight economy, service providers must venture into the invisible market to become a preferred or sole provider. This is best achieved by finding and then aligning to a prospect's Transformation MVP.

Value mining in the invisible market means overcoming your fear of rejection. It requires gaining access, seeking mutual understanding and articulating your MVP-aligned service value. It means using an MVP Questioning Strategy to build and assess motivation for change, to build clarity and consensus for a shared vision, and to reduce resistance to your proposed solution path. It means aligning and presenting your recommendations to the prospect's decision stage and MVP.

Preference Value Mining in the visible market means understating and articulating your rational preference value to survive the screening phase and then demonstrating your understanding of the client and your commitment to the project to build emotional preference to win the business. Finally, by Value Mining with all client stakeholders across an organization, you will win the engagement and win the relationship.

I don't believe you can become proficient in Value Mining by spending a couple of hours reading this book any more than I believe you can win the British Open by reading *Golf Magazine*. Service selling at the executive level is an extremely complex interaction with unlimited variations. A book that would try to capture it all would collapse under its own weight.

Mastery comes with time, diligence, review and practice. But you need help now, so let me give you a few quick tips that will work for you immediately.

"Just Do It"

Get in front of the client. Even if you don't do it well, there is no substitute for this type of direct interaction. Remember that service providers who have not experienced a down market vastly underestimate the amount of face-to-face time needed to succeed.

Build a basic business development plan that converts long-term revenue goals into daily action plans by breaking down revenue targets into number of engagements, number of proposals that lead to engagements, number of face-to-face calls per proposal, number of face-to-face calls to reach a proposal and number of phone calls to gain access to a prospect. By doing so, you will get a more realistic view of the time you will need to allocate to business development efforts.

Bring An Attitude of Enlightened Self-Interest:
How to Approach Face-to-Face Meetings

You get what you want only if the client gets what he or she wants, so forget everything that you have read here while you are with the prospect. Your only concern is to help the prospect optimally align to his or her market. Forget your solutions, your Service Value Chart and your Preference Value Chart. It's all about the prospective client. Anything that distracts you from focusing on and listening to the prospect undermines trust. If you are thinking about what Potter told you to do next, you are not engaged. There will be plenty of time to review and plan when you are not face-to-face with the prospect.

When You Feel the Urge to Talk:
Ask Three More Questions

I suppose it is possible to ask too many questions, but given the natural propensity to show your expertise, I would advise you to err on the side of asking more. This will help you avoid the Premature Solution Syndrome as well as help you get in sync and stay in sync with your prospect. Focus on winning the engagement, not winning the business.

That's it! Now, go build your value charts. And make that call – today.

About The Author

Robert A. Potter is the managing principal of RA Potter Advisors, a marketing and sales strategy consulting practice serving professional service providers. Bob spent 25 years in sales and business development for IBM, McGraw-Hill, Dean Witter and MBIA. He has opened new markets in the U.S., Mexico, Australia and Asia. He received his B.A. degree from Santa Clara University and his M.B.A from UC Berkeley. He lives with his wife and sons in San Anselmo, CA.

Bob is a frequent speaker and writer on the topic. If you would like more information, please go to: www.rapotter.com or contact Bob at:

RA Potter Advisors
bpotter@rapotter.com